ON TRIUMPH

1967-1972

Reprinted From
Cycle World Magazine

ISBN 1 869826 582

Published By
Brooklands Books with permission of Cycle World

Titles in this series

CYCLE WORLD ON BMW 1964-1973
CYCLE WORLD ON BMW 1974-1980
CYCLE WORLD ON BMW 1981-1986
CYCLE WORLD ON BSA 1962-1971
CYCLE WORLD ON DUCATI 1962-1980
CYCLE WORLD ON DUCATI 1982-1991
CYCLE WORLD ON HARLEY-DAVIDSON 1962-1968
CYCLE WORLD ON HARLEY-DAVIDSON 1968-1978
CYCLE WORLD ON HARLEY-DAVIDSON 1978-1983
CYCLE WORLD ON HARLEY-DAVIDSON 1983-1987
CYCLE WORLD ON HARLEY-DAVIDSON 1987-1990
CYCLE WORLD ON HARLEY-DAVIDSON 1990-1992
CYCLE WORLD ON HONDA 1962-1967
CYCLE WORLD ON HONDA 1968-1971
CYCLE WORLD ON HONDA 1971-1974
CYCLE WORLD ON HUSQVANA 1966-1976
CYCLE WORLD ON HUSQVANA 1977-1984
CYCLE WORLD ON KAWASAKI 1966-1971
CYCLE WORLD ON KAWASAKI OFF-ROAD BIKES 1972-1976
CYCLE WORLD ON KAWASAKI STREET BIKES 1972-1976
CYCLE WORLD ON NORTON 1962-1971
CYCLE WORLD ON TRIUMPH 1962-1967
CYCLE WORLD ON TRIUMPH 1967-1972
CYCLE WORLD ON TRIUMPH 1972-1987
CYCLE WORLD ON SUZUKI 1967-1970
CYCLE WORLD ON SUZUKI OFF-ROAD BIKES 1971-1976
CYCLE WORLD ON SUZUKI STREET BIKES 1971-1976
CYCLE WORLD ON YAMAHA 1962-1969
CYCLE WORLD ON YAMAHA OFF-ROAD BIKES 1970-1974
CYCLE WORLD ON YAMAHA STREET BIKES 1970-1974

DISTRIBUTED BY

CarTech,
11481 Kost Dam Road,
North Branch,
MN 55056, USA
Phone: 800 551 4754 & 612 583 3471
Fax: 612 583 2023

Brooklands Books Ltd.,
1/81 Darley St.,
PO Box 199, Mona Vale,
NSW 2103, Australia
Phone: 2 997 8428
Fax: 2 452 4679

Brooklands Books Ltd,
PO Box 146,
Cobham, Surrey KT11 1LG
England
Phone: 0932 865051
Fax: 0932 868803

We are frequently asked for copies of out of print Road Tests and other articles that have appeared in Cycle World. To satisfy this need we are producing a series of books that will include, as nearly as possible, all the important information on one make or subject for a given period.

It is our hope that these collections of articles will give an overview that will be of value to historians, restorers and potential buyers, as well as to present owners of these interesting motorcycles.

TRIUMPH T100R
DAYTONA

A Cafe Racer's Dream

MOTORCYCLE MANUFACTURERS have long displayed a penchant for naming their products in honor of a major race or event, particularly after having experienced some success in the event whose name is chosen to grace a line model. Often as not, a grandly christened new machine bears little resemblance, other than physical, to the number that did the job. It was no great surprise that Triumph, following their smashing Daytona victory last year, would offer a 500cc twin dubbed "Daytona." What is surprising — and pleasantly so — is that the new model, despite its handsome but not too hairy roadster appearance, is closely related to the machine that Buddy Elmore rode to the checkers.

The most noteworthy improvement in the 1967 Triumph 500 is the steering geometry — very closely approximating that of Triumph's previous 650s. In combination with the gusseted swing arm pivot, this has produced a superb handling roadster. Happily, the Daytona retains its very desirable "around town" nimbleness, and even in snail-pace, stop-and-go traffic, the bike never seems clumsy and out of place.

Triumph has retained its single-loop frame for '67, but has increased top- and down-tube diameters. There is little doubt that this, too, has contributed to improved handling.

The front forks remain basically unchanged. Travel is more than sufficient and damping is good. The steering is always responsive and confident. On striated freeway surfaces the front end evidenced little wander, and it is possible to cinch the friction steering damper down to cause this to disappear altogether. Rear spring-shock units are, of course, Girling. Their three-way adjustment does a fairly decent job of permitting them to function properly with a wide range of passenger and baggage load.

The most obvious change in the powerplant for the new 500 is in carburetion. The twin 1-1/8-inch Amals allow the engine to breathe comfortably at high speed and are anything but intractable at the bottom end of the scale. In fact, blipping the throttle with the engine untaxed and at idle produces crisp, rapid rev rises, unmarked with spitting and hesitation. Internally, the Daytona sports some new items, such as true hemispherical combustion chambers in place of the previous stepped squish chambers. Also, a new oil pump with a higher capacity scavenge has been added this year. With the new combustion chamber the 500 has received a two-degree reduction in included valve angle, producing a more desirable rocker-to-valve relationship. In support of the axiom that "racing improves the breed," we mention that the changes covered so far were first seen on last year's Daytona 200 winner.

Breathing has been further improved on the Daytona through the addition of Q-type exhaust cams. Previously, the 500 used only Q intake cams. Also, Triumph's R-radius followers have been employed to realize increased duration, and the diameter of the intake valves has been increased to 1-17/32 inches.

The power characteristics of the Daytona exhibit a real Jekyl-and-Hyde personality. When taken no higher than 4,500 rpm, the engine works like a very strong thirty-fifty — very healthy, very satisfying — and it would probably be possible to ride the machine in this manner throughout its life without being disappointed in its performance. If you choose instead to hesitate just an instant before making a 4,500-rpm gear change you are in for a surprise, because it's at this point that the bike starts to "get legs." Once the effective cam design range has been experienced, it's difficult to muster enough discipline to make gear changes at anything less than 6,000 rpm. This delightful madness is still further encouraged by the close-ratio gearbox which keeps the engine "on range" during the trip up to fourth.

We were mightily impressed with the performance of the gearbox throughout the test program. The bike was used for to-work-and-back transportation, for highway jaunts, and then wrung out at Riverside raceway during timed acceleration and top-end runs, and always, the gearbox performed as though it had been designed specifically for each of these widely differing duties. The transmission is a strange combination of precision, super-heavy-duty and lightness of throw that has one — count it — one neutral that is always easily found. And, if the rider is ever in doubt that he is in neutral, he need only look down at the right-side engine case to read the gear indicator. We would be inclined to take Triumph to task on the placement of the indicator, which must be searched for, if the selector action were not so precise.

The Daytona maintains its ancestral legend when it

TRIUMPH T100R DAYTONA

SPECIFICATIONS

List price	$1199
Suspension, front	telescopic fork
Suspension, rear	swing arm
Tire, front	3.25-19
Tire, rear	4.00-18
Brake, front	7 x 1.13
Brake, rear	7 x 1.13
Total brake swept area, sq.-in.	49.7
Brake loading (test weight/swept area) lb/sq-in.	10.6
Engine type	ohv, vertical twin
Bore and stroke (inches-millimeters)	2.72 x 2.58, 69 x 65.5
Displacement (inches^3-centimeters^3)	30, 490
Compression ratio	9:1
Carburetion	Amal Monobloc (2), 1-1/16"
Ignition	energy transfer
Bhp @ rpm	41 @ 7,200
Oil system	dry sump
Oil capacity, pts.	6
Fuel capacity, gal.	3.3
Starting system	kick, folding crank
Lighting system	alternator and battery
Air filtration	paper element
Clutch	multi-disc, wet plate
Primary drive	duplex chain
Final drive	single-row chain
Gear ratios, overall:1	
5th	none
4th	5.4
3rd	6.6
2nd	8.7
1st	13.4
Wheelbase	54.5
Seat height	31.5
Seat width	11.0
Foot-peg height	12.5
Ground clearance	7.0
Curb weight (w/half-tank fuel)	371
Test weight (fuel and rider)	531

PERFORMANCE

Top speed	105
Maximum speed in gears (@ 7800 rpm)	
5th	none
4th	111
3rd	91
2nd	68
1st	40
Mph per 1000 rpm, top gear	14.2
Speedometer error	
30 mph indicated, actually	32.1
50	52.6
70	72.9
Acceleration, zero to	
30 mph, sec.	3.4
40	4.4
50	5.8
60	7.0
70	9.3
80	11.6
90	14.9
100	21.3
Standing 1/8-mile, sec.	9.6
terminal speed	72
Standing 1/4-mile, sec.	14.9
terminal speed	90

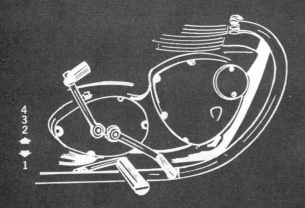

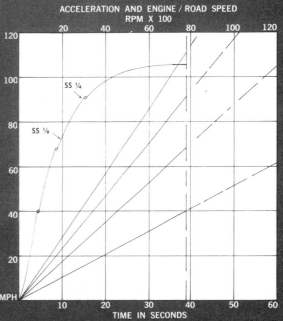

ACCELERATION AND ENGINE / ROAD SPEED
RPM X 100

comes time to bring the engine to life. Nothing, but *nothing,* is easier to start than a Triumph twin, and the only "problem" experienced was brought about by an initial reluctance to top off the float chamber for the twin Amals. When the tickler has been held down long enough to produce a spurt from the overfull vent, the engine will start with the first kick — without the aid of chokes — no matter how long it has remained idle. On cold mornings, the engine arrives at operating temperature rather quickly. We were convinced, in fact, that it could be started and ridden away immediately, although, in deference to the engine's lubrication requirements, we would not recommend this.

The brakes on the Daytona must get a "more than adequate" nod. They quickly pull the machine down from speed, and for intended use, are nigh fade-proof. Most of the time, the rear stopper is wholly adequate, and in panic situations, or when cafe-racing, the front and rear in combination haul the bike down like a pitched-out anchor.

While the tire selection for the Daytona is fairly standard practice for English roadsters — Dunlop rib in front and K70 Gold Seal in back — they feel as though they couldn't be better if they had been designed with this chassis in mind.

In the electrical department, this bike is one of the best. Triumph has been working long and hard with their supplier to provide a truly proper system and it appears that the effort has paid off. Lighting is excellent. The headlight is strong enough to reach out and illuminate unexpected hazards; instrument lights keep you abreast of road speed and revs; indicators tell you that the ignition switch is turned to "on" and your high beam is operating; and the strong taillight-stoplight combination gives you confidence that you won't be run down by an overtaking auto. We feel that it is significant to mention that Triumph was one of the first manufacturers to have their electrical systems accepted by law enforcement agencies in this country. We are curious, however, that they were able to receive a stamp of approval for their unquestionably feeble horn; this item would pass a public library annoyance test with flying colors! However, we have seen horns of this design that do work.

The hinged dualseat, brand-new to Triumph's 500s this year, is just about unequaled in comfort and, thus far, one of the best aesthetic approaches to fanny platforms we've seen. We won't hazard a guess at how many hours of contemplation and design time have gone into this saddle, but we know that they are many; one doesn't simply arrive at this sort of solution by accident. We're torn in our evaluation of the sports-style gas tank. The design is excellent and we particularly like the slim knee pads. But the parcel rack has been scrubbed for this model. One can live with the cruising range offered by the 3.3-gallon fuel capacity, but not with the fact that one has only two miles to get to a gas station after the reserve has been switched on (the bike does push rather easily, as we pleasantly found out).

Rider position is quite good for the average sized person. The narrow roadster bars are best appreciated after several hours in the saddle. They are wide enough to allow you to maneuver in big-city traffic with a great deal of control, but are sufficiently narrow to be comfortable at sustained high speeds. Triumph has seen fit to go to spongy grips this year, and while they are just dandy with bare hands, they are uncomfortably sloppy with gloves. And while we're concerning ourselves with gloves, we wish to state that all of the Daytona's controls, from the gas cocks to the dipper switch, can easily be handled by insulated-glove hands.

To be counted among its most endearing qualities as a roadster, is the Daytona's noise level. It makes just enough noise to let you know that it is alive and kicking. It has, of course, that typical, and most pleasant, Triumph rumble. The exhaust note is mild enough not to offend the automobile types, but is sufficiently right to excite those who know "where it's at."

In the quality-of-finish department one will search long and hard before he is able to produce an equal to Triumph motorcycles. The Daytona, of course, is no exception to this most pleasant tradition. The bike is superbly crafted and, in a word, beautiful.

The Triumph T100R Daytona clearly reflects its enviable heritage. It's a well-bred mount that will graphically illustrate how its sporty brother so handily won the premier crown in American road racing last year. ∎

TRIUMPH®'67
A New Experience in Motorcycling

TRIUMPH® **presents the Champi**

*New power, new performance,
in the great tradition of the
world's best and fastest motorcycle*

It's an exciting year. O
high-performance mot
improved acceleration
bold, modern look, fro
And with sales at an e
See the Championship

T120R — Bonneville Road Sports
Twin Carburetors/40 cu. in. (650 c.c.)

Here is the fastest standard motorcycle in the world today. Strictly for the expert rider. Color: Burgundy Red and Alaskan White. Polished stainless steel fenders.

T120TT — Bonneville TT Special
Twin Carburetors/40 cu. in. (650 c.c.)

Winner of more TT races than all other makes combined. For competition riding only. Color: Burgundy Red and Alaskan White.

ship Line for '67

Triumph moves out front with a great new line of
For 1967, an impressive array of new design features:
arting, better performance at high speeds. And a
ers to the new colors that set Triumph apart for '67.
gh, never was there a better year to Go Triumph.
1967. At your Triumph Dealer's now.

T20M — Mountain Cub
200 c.c. Lightweight

Top lightweight on the market today. 4 cycle OHV. Single cylinder. At home in the woods or on the road. Color: Grenadier Red and White.

TR6R — Trophy Road Sports
Single Carburetor/40 cu. in. (650 c.c.)

The top long distance machine, perfect for touring and everyday riding. Color: Mist Green and White.

TR6C — Trophy Competition
Single Carburetor/40 cu. in. (650 c.c.)

Versatility Plus! A proven winner in Enduros and cross-country events, yet ideal for on-the-road riding. Color: Mist Green and White.

T100R — Daytona Super Sports
Twin Carburetors/30.5 cu. in. (500 c.c.)

Latest addition to the Triumph line. Named for the Triumph that won Daytona's 200-mile National Championship Road Race in 1966. Color: Pacific Blue and White.

T100C — Sports Tiger
Single Carburetor/30.5 cu. in. (500 c.c.)

A competition bike that excels on road or trail. Agile, with quick power and steady performance. Color: Pacific Blue and White.

TRIUMPH® *is a Way of Life*

Ride a Triumph for the first time and you'll never be the same again. You'll do things. Go places. Your world will open up to let adventure in. And why not? A Triumph just naturally wants to be on the move. The extra power and built-in high performance of a Triumph will lead you to a new level of fun and excitement. Come along for the ride. See your Triumph dealer soon.

Triumph — holder of the A.M.A. approved NEW WORLD'S SPEED RECORD, Bonneville, Utah, 245.667 m.p.h. (with streamlined shell).

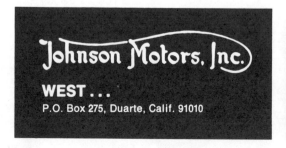

Write for FREE catalog in full color and name of dealer nearest you. Dept. Z.

THROUGHOUT ITS HISTORY, motorcycling has had its magic product names. The like of JAP, Manx, Gilera Four, Amal GP and Goldstar have earned their respected positions not through press-agentry, but through performance. A new name has been added to the list in recent years — Metisse — and like the other marques, its revered position has been earned.

In the last year or so, American scrambles riders have become increasingly aware of the Metisse story, but mainly the exposure has been indirect, through articles or seeing one in action. A very fortunate few have had the unforgettable experience of riding one of the several that have been brought to the U.S. It now looks like more of us will get the chance, because the Rickman-Metisse is now available to American riders. Appropriately enough, the man responsible for importing the wonder-chassis is one of this country's most capable scrambles and hare-and-hound riders — Bud Ekins. Ekins, in addition to his competence as a racer, has been one of the nation's leading Triumph dealers for the past 13 years. All of this dovetails neatly with his contacts and friendships with English racers and builders, made during his ISDT and scrambles campaigns abroad.

For some months, CYCLE WORLD has known of Bud's plans, but because of the tenuous nature of pre-contract agreements and the knotty problems involved in importing a new product, we elected to remain mum until the bird was firmly in hand. From the time he had cemented the importing arrangement until our interview — a period measured in weeks — Bud has charged as hard and fast in his new venture as he does on a race course. His Yankee-prepared Metisses have seen several outings and garnered two significant victories — first places in the Open Expert class at both the Ensenada and Hopetown GPs.

In our interview with Bud, we endeav-

EKINS'
TRIUMPH
METISSE

ored to discover and subsequently present not a history of the Metisse, nor an academic dissertation of the chassis' geometry, but, instead, a detailed picture of how the purchasable item is put together, and what parts and components are used, and the reasons for their selection.

CYCLE WORLD: *For openers, how about giving us an outline of the basic ingredients for one of your Metisses?*

EKINS: Well, I start with a Rickman-Metisse kit, Ceriani fork legs, BSA fork stem, crown, and bearing races, a pile of Triumph parts that cover better than 10 model years and either a 500 or 650 Triumph unit engine. The kit, by the way, differs slightly for each engine.

CW: *Let's break it down further and see what the kit is made up of.*

EKINS: The Metisse kit comprises the frame, rear swing arm with chain adjuster cams, handle bars — which, by the way, are excellent — exhaust pipes, foot pegs, brake arm, still-air box and air cleaners, engine mounting plates, gas tank, seat frame, seat, fenders, mid-section side panels and all the self-locking nuts and bolts needed to put the kit together.

CW: *What's your feeling about the manufacturing integrity of the Rickman-Metisse kit — does it require a lot of heating and bending to get the parts to line up?*

EKINS: The kit's excellent. The piece drop into place — within reason, of course

CW: *Within reason?*

EKINS: Yes. I've yet to see even a production motorcycle disassembled and reassembled without using rawhide and bronze mallets. The Metisse is no exception to this, but I've yet to resort to heat to get things to line up.

CW: *How are the fiberglass components to work with?*

EKINS: They're beautiful, really. The glass work is done by Avon and is some of the best around. Not only do the glass components fit perfectly, but they're super light, super-strong, and beautifully detail

PHOTOS BY DAVID GOOLEY

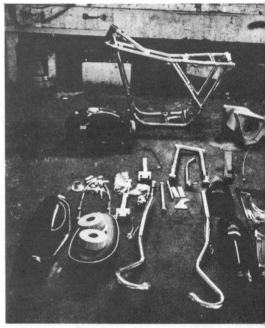

ed. The colors are in the gel coat and hold up much better than paint. I'm only bringing in two colors, BRG and red. The Rickman's have two others — ivory and blue. But, tetraethyl stains the ivory and the blue is dumb!

CW: So much for the kit. How about the other components, like the front suspension?

EKINS: Well, as I've said, I use Ceriani fork legs and BSA stem, crown, and bearing races.

CW: Why not the Ceriani components? Aren't they lighter and easier to work with?

EKINS: Whether or not the Ceriani parts are significantly lighter than the BSA is debatable. But, let's forget about weight and take a look at geometry. The Rickmans designed their chassis with European motocross in mind — understandably. For the most part, their courses are slower than ours in the straights. Relative to what they ride, we ride three-dimensional speedway. Now, we can take this one step further and throw in hare-and-hounds, where speeds approaching 100 mph are not uncommon for the front runners. Imagine trying to handle unimproved terrain at that speed with flattrack-type steering geometry! The BSA "triple clamps" give the fork stanchions about 1-1/2 degrees less inclination than the steering head and greatly slow down the steering. In addition, rear end response, or whip, is less violent.

CW: We note with some interest that your lashup doesn't use a U-brace between the fork legs. Don't you feel that this might be a good device to add?

EKINS: The U-brace is a poor solution to the problem of keeping forks true, because it increases unsprung weight. I feel that the simplest solution is to braze a piece of tubing on each side of the fork crowns, as I do to the Metisses, saw through the tubing and the stanchion hole, and then fit a pinch bolt into the tubing. Not only does this permit me to cinch the

stanchions so they maintain constant relationship, but it also allows me to move the stanchions up and down to increase or decrease trail.

CW: Are there any other changes that you make to the BSA triple clamps?

EKINS: One other. I drill out the pinch-bolt holes in the bottom bridge and use the larger Triumph pinch bolt.

CW: That pretty much satisfies us in regard to the suspension, but while we're on this end of the machine, let's find out what you do about a front wheel.

EKINS: I use a mixture of components for the front wheel. I start with a pre-1954 Triumph hub, which is light and strong, add '64 or later Triumph floating rear brake shoes, and lace the assembly to a WM-2 19-inch Akront alloy rim with standard Triumph spokes.

CW: Why not play it safe and use heavy-duty spokes?

EKINS: They're unnecessary with the Metisse. You've got to remember that we're dealing with a totally different concept here than we're accustomed to. Much of the old "technology" is useless and when you examine it closely you discover that it involved modifications to correct the shortcomings of bikes that were not inherently suited to high speeds on cobby ground. With the Metisse, the opposite is true; it was designed for rough work. I'd like to add, at this point, that if you wish to be successful with a Metisse, you've got to believe in it. If you mess around with wheelbase or weight bias or head angle or anything else involving changes to the overall chassis geometry, simply because these factors "just don't seem right," you are going to wind up with a nearly useless machine that's going to put you on your head everytime you relax.

CW: One more thing before we get into the back wheel. What size and type tire do you put on the front?

EKINS: I use a 3.50-19 Dunlop Trials Universal. Normally, you would expect to

see a 4.00-19 fitted, but the forks aren't wide enough to take it and it's really unnecessary unsprung weight with this chassis.

For the rear wheel I use a standard '66 Triumph hub because it takes a bolt-on sprocket instead of an overlay. I machine bearing spacers from alloy and use the Rickman axle which is supplied with the kit. I lace the hub into an 18-inch WM-3 Akront rim and mount a 4.00-18 Dunlop Sports.

CW: We seem to have covered just about everything but the engine. What modifications do you make to an engine before installing it in the chassis?

EKINS: I *can* make any number of modifications that are considered SOP for Triumph competition engines. But I prefer to leave them stock. A Metisse with either a standard 500 or 650 Triumph unit engine is considerably faster than a hot twin in a standard chassis. The power gained from speed mods is not only unnecessary, but generally drops overall dependability.

CW: Is there any special equipment required to build a Triumph-Metisse?

EKINS: Other than a lathe to turn bearing and exhaust pipe spacers and a press to fit the bushings into the swing arm, the bike can be assembled with standard hand tools. The lathe and press work is pretty easy to job out to a small machine shop at a reasonable price, if a builder doesn't have access to the equipment.

CW: How much time is involved in building the bike?

EKINS: Realistically, we're talking about 24 to 30 hours, depending on the builder's ability.

CW: What sort of curb weight figures are you coming up with?

EKINS: The 650 Metisse, with a gallon of gas and four quarts of oil, weighs 298 pounds; the 500 weighs 283.

CW: What is the cost of a Metisse and what's the most reasonable approach to take?

EKINS: First, the most reasonable approach is to supply your own bike — a complete, late-model Triumph 500 or 650. Then, you either purchase the kit and all the ingredients we've talked about for $950 and build your own, or I'll build it for you for $1000.

CW: The $50 difference seems like a real bargain for having you do the work!

EKINS: Yes, I guess you could say it is, but it works out well for me, too, because if I build the bike I retain all the salvage. And, actually, the leftover standard chassis parts aren't much use to the owner — it's pretty certain that he isn't going to go back to a standard model after he's spent some time on a Metisse.

CW: As a rider, what do you think of the Triumph-Metisse combinations?

EKINS: It's an excellent machine. It's easy and fun to ride and doesn't tire you quickly when you're really pressing. Handling is great. The bike's responsive, steady and doesn't snake or whip. All in all, it's a tough one to beat. As an indication of the regard European motocross riders have for the Metisse, let me say that conservative estimates put the number of Rickman-Metisse chassis on European and English starting grids at about 60 percent, and about 90 percent of the bikes making it to the winner's circle are Metisse! ∎

CYCLE WORLD
ROAD TEST

M**ANY MOTORCYCLES** have their counterparts in the automotive world — the temperamental, expensive but very fast types, the comfortable and quiet long-distance tourers. Well, then, why not a two-wheel counterpart for the funny little car that is always the same while constantly improving. If ever there was a motorcycle that could be considered to remain the same, year after year, while constantly improving, it would be the Triumph Tiger Cub.

The mini-thumper from Coventry has long been a favorite of many American lightweight-class scrambles and TT racers, but in its homeland, it is generally thought of as "trials iron." Indeed, it is a good trialer, and particularly so when fitted with optional trials trappings, such as foot pegs, saddle, bars and the like. The Trials Cub is not readily available in the U.S., however. The model tested was, instead, the more familiar Mountain version, which, even without the special bits, is a respectable trialer.

The frame of the Cub is a two-piece affair, utilizing forged junctions. It is beautifully finished and lacks the "cobbiness" usually found in frames with fabricated junctions. The fuel tank has two internal stiffeners, which assist the single top tube, but does not require a space con-

suming tunnel to allow for a second top tube.

Suspension is one of the Cub's strong points. The front forks are only slightly scaled down from the units Triumph use on their big twins. As such, these forks have ample travel and good damping. The bridge and crown are sturdy steel forgings and do an excellent job of keeping the fork legs parallel. Girling lightweight spring-shocks are used in the rear, and experience tells us that there isn't a better unit made for this chassis, regardless of the intended use. The Cub's short wheelbase and moderate head angle are well suited to slow, pick-your-way riding and yet are quite civilized at speed on rough ground.

Most of the Cub's appeal must surely be credited to its engine. This was Triumph's first unit-construction engine and has always been a tidy package. It puts out considerable torque for its size, and this over a very broad band, making it one of the more tractable lightweight performers. Small, four-stroke singles are generally regarded as interesting toys, but this is one powerplant that makes no bones about being an honest-to-goodness motorcycle engine. At its present stage of development, the Cub engine is sturdy, and this is the product of increased finning

with consequential temperature reduction, increased oil pump capacity, ball bearing mains and — of course — years of refinement.

The Cub's power is transmitted through a duplex chain and cork-faced multi-plate clutch (with a rubber cush-drive) to a wide-ratio gearbox that is one of the smoothest, most positive on the market. Selector throw is light, short and consistent, adding to rider confidence and precluding a shortened temper. Combined with a pleasantly light clutch control lever, the entire task of getting the power onto the ground is wholly satisfactory.

Triumph must be congratulated on the electrics in the Cub. The AC/DC ignition/lighting arrangement — *sans* battery — is often unsatisfactory, for one reason or another, like hard starting or dim lights at low speed, but Triumph seems to have come up with a system that is completely satisfactory; the Cub starts easily, even after having sat for a day or so, and the lights are bright, even at idle. All in all, what with quickly detachable headlight, hearty vibrator horn and kill button, the system is completely reasonable.

With regard to trials riding, we feel that the Cub is

TRIUMPH TIGER CUB

potentially quite good. Specifically, as tested, we were plagued with several annoyances. The standard pegs are mounted too low and too far forward for a comfortable and controllable standing position and in combination with the stock bars, which are narrow and pulled back too far, the bike is tiring to ride — particularly so on steep ascents. The standard twinseat is much larger than necessary for a trailer. The Cub's potentially good steering lock is hindered by long stop bolts, and when these are shortened, the forks bottom on the tank.

It may seem unfair that we are evaluating a trail bike as a trialer and thus have an inordinate amount of criticisms, but we have reason to approach the bike in this manner; trials riding is growing quickly in this country and the Cub deserves the chance to prove that it is one of the best machines for this sport and that chance will have to come through increased availability of the necessary components. As we've said, the Cub is potentially quite good; its torque characteristics are to be envied by anyone building a trialer. The engine will throttle down to a murmur, motor along at this rate for as long as one wishes, and then wind right back up when there is a slope to be tackled. The engine is in a relatively mild state of tune, and, therefore, rarely needs clutching and cleaning out. Throttle response is not bad, but the 15/16-inch Amal Monobloc is a compromise in favor of higher speeds than normally found in trials.

As a trials chassis, the Cub is good — quite good, in fact. Steering is precise, despite the 19-inch front wheel. The bike has a very low c.g. and particularly so for a four-stroke with its topside valve gear. Top hamper is low and width is minimal while still offering good grip at the tank.

The exhaust system is robust but not unpleasantly raucous. Several hours of riding in trials fashion netted no noise fatigue. The exhaust system, incidentally, reflects the Cub's over-the-years refinement; not only is it reasonably quiet, but it is tucked well out of the way and will not damage the rider's exterior, nor is it susceptible to damage from rocks and other sundry obstacles.

The Cub has two features that are particularly endearing to the rider who handles his own maintenance; the ignition point-breaker assembly is readily accessible, located beneath a quickly removed plate on the right-side engine cover, and the clutch cable end is simply reached through a rubber-plugged access port in the same cover. This latter item should hold special appeal for owners of early Cubs who were faced with the task of removing the gear selector, starter and entire right cover to gain access to the cable.

Finish work on the Cub is typically Triumph — excellent. Painted surfaces are generously and handsomely covered. Plating is without flaw and detailing of the aluminum is excellent. The overall finish and appearance belies the retail price of the bike and is hardly to be expected, even on machinery selling for several hundred more.

In standard form, the Cub is an excellent dual-purpose woods and street motorcycle that can be ridden comfortably for hours at a stretch. For the serious trialsman, its shortcomings will need some attention, and all of them can be simply and inexpensively remedied, either through the use of off-the-shelf items or "home-brewed" modifications. For either application, it is worthy of some very serious consideration.

TRIUMPH CUB

SPECIFICATIONS

List price	$675
Suspension, front	telescopic
Suspension, rear	swing arm
Tire size, front	3.00-19
Tire size, rear	3.50-18
Engine type	ohv., single
Bore and stroke (″-mm)	2.48x2.52, 63 x 64
Displacement, cu. in.	12.2
Displacement, cu. cent.	199
Bhp @ rpm	16 @ 6,800
Carburetion	Amal Monobloc,15/16 in.
Ignition	A.C. magneto
Fuel capacity, gal.	2.5
Oil capacity, pts.	2.75
Oil system	dry sump
Starting system	kick, folding crank

POWER TRANSMISSION

Clutch type	multi-disc, wet plate
Primary drive	duplex chain
Final drive	single-row chain
Gear ratio, overall:1	
5th	none
4th	9.58
3rd	14.22
2nd	22.25
1st	32.25

DIMENSION, INCHES

Wheelbase	51.0
Saddle height	32.0
Saddle width	11.5
Footpeg height	10.5
Ground clearance	8.0
Curb weight	243

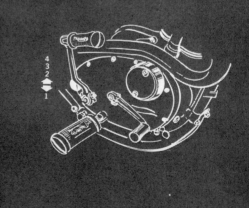

THE TRIUMPH FACTORY stopped taking an active interest in racing almost 18 years ago when the Triumph Grand Prix project came to an end. But American tuners, being what they are, saw an engine that lent itself to home tuning; one that could be very competitive under AMA rules. And through the years, the 500 Triumph can boast a staggering list of successes in this country. All of this has been done with American speed accessories, from special crankshafts to racing valve springs.

This changed somewhat when the Triumph factory obtained Doug Hele, a first class engineer who is more than a little interested in racing. One of Doug's first tasks was to develop a new fork for street Triumphs, an easy chore for someone who had worked on forks for the world's famous racing Nortons. To say the new front end helped the handling would be an understatement — it was a transformation. From that point on, the street Triumphs have become more sophisticated in almost every respect.

Frame and engine modifications were made for last year's Daytona races, and shortly afterwards, the T100 R was made available to the public. The machine incorporated almost all of the design innovations used in Buddy Elmore's motorcycle. The Triumphs this year were quicker, handled better, and were certainly much smaller than any previous Coventry five-hundred.

To get a better look at the machine, we asked to take one to Riverside. We wanted Gary Nixon's winning mount. However, it will be in Baltimore, Gary's home base. Instead, we were offered Dick Hamner's ride, which suited us just fine, for it was the fastest Triumph in qualifying. It required a new fairing and a little straightening here and there, due to Dick's 100 mph prang, but other than that, it was in remarkable condition.

Probably the most creditable thing about the six factory prepared Triumphs, apart from the 1-2 finish, is that all six of them finished the race, and that all of them were running as well at the end as they were on the first lap. We managed a look inside one of the engines at Daytona, and found that it has a squish-type combustion chamber, quite similar to the Manx Norton arrangement. Piston to head clearance in the squish area is .030 ± .003, again similar to the Manx.

Most of the changes have been made to

TRIUMPH DAYTONA RACER ★

Jomo's service manager, Al Stucky (left) and assistant Pat Owens share a laugh with the editor.

the cycle parts. Probably the largest single contributor to improved lap times was the new Fontana four leading shoe front brake. All of the riders liked it, once they had recovered from the shock of having the front wheel stop if the brake was used without discretion. In fact, it's the sort of brake that can be operated all the way with two fingers, or very gingerly with four. A standard Triumph rear brake is used on the back.

The Triumphs last year had very low frontal area, which sent everyone scurrying home to whittle their fairings. But this year, the machines were even smaller; in fact, as small as most of the 250 production racers in physical size. This was accomplished by fitting 18-inch wheels in place of the standard 19-inch that English racing machines have always used. Also, the front forks were shortened by cutting 1 inch from the top of the stanchions and sliding them up further into the fork crowns. A corresponding amount was removed from the fork springs to maintain the correct poundage.

Except for the kink in the right side member, to allow the exhaust pipe to pass inside, the frame has not been altered in any way. It is exactly the same frame used on the Daytona street model. Last year's ugly gas tank and seat have been replaced by very appealing units from Birmingham Fiberglass Mouldings. Now the rider can get down much lower, with considerably more comfort. The fairing is also much smaller than before, and all of the fiberglass components are surprisingly lightweight. The whole machine only weighs 301 pounds with a half tank of gas.

Externally, the engine does not appear to have changed greatly. The large radially finned exhaust pipe clamps have been replaced by plain, unfinned bands, to improve the airflow to the heads. All of the rear exhaust pipe mounts have rubber bushes, and are actually quite flexible. The carburetor arrangement is quite unusual, although it has been used on some of the European multis. An Amal flat-type float chamber is mounted between the two 1-3/16 Amal GPs. However, it is not hung on an adjustable rod; instead, the banjo outlet spigots are set at 180° and hook up rigidly to the carburetor inlet fitting. This means that the float chamber is fixed relative to the carburetors, and everything must be right in the beginning, as they cannot be adjusted. The advantage is that they cannot come unadjusted, either!

To prevent fuel frothing and all of the evils connected with rigid float chambers, the hoses between the carburetors and cylinderhead spigots are quite flexible. Two U-shaped brackets on the main frame downtube support the carburetor bells on rubber pads.

The oil lines have now been routed over the top of the gearbox, rather than underneath, to permit the right side exhaust pipe to tuck in close to the engine unit. More and more machines racing in the AMA are incorporating oil radiators. The main reason is that, under AMA rules, basic engine castings must be used. And, although

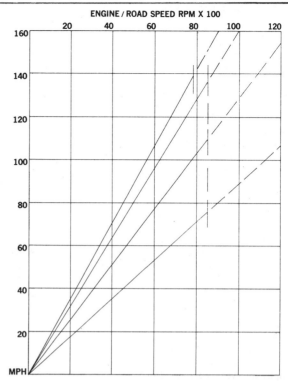

ENGINE / ROAD SPEED RPM X 100

cylinder and head finning may be ample for any touring requirements, it may be a marginal situation under prolonged hard racing. If the oil temperature can be kept down, it will act as a coolant and carry heat away. Daytona Triumphs, like last year, are fitted with a Chevrolet Corvair oil cooler.

Even from cold, the Triumph started well, although the oil cooler did prolong the warmup time considerably. First gear is slightly higher than second on the street counterpart, and it might be expected, with a highly tuned racing engine, to require considerable clutch slip to get underway. However, an extremely wide power band makes the task an easy one. In fact, as we see it, the really good torque characteristics of the engine contributed much to the machine's phenomenal success at Daytona. The machine can be ridden at anything over 4,500 rpm, and from 6,000 rpm to

red line, things happen very quickly, particularly in first and second gears. A good habit, when racing Triumphs, is to shift from first at least 500 revs below red line because once the engine gets near peak in first, it can climb the last 500 revs in one second, near enough.

With Daytona gearing, Riverside Raceway becomes a very small course, indeed. Turn nine to turn one is virtually an S bend. The rear springs were set up too far initially, causing chop over the bumps at turn one; but setting them to the softest position sorted the handling out very well.

It can be said without reservation that the new Triumph is on par or better than anything else for handling, and that includes Manxes, G50s, 7Rs, Honda 4, last year's Triumph racer and various other racing equipment ridden at Riverside.

What a great production racer it would make!

A LOOK AT
DOUG HELE

TRIUMPH'S DEVELOPMENT ENGINEE

BY B. R. NICHOLLS

"**S**UCCESS IS one percent inspiration ar 99 percent perspiration." So says book marker sent by Al Stuckey, P. Owens and Jack Wilson of Johnson Moto to the occupant of a first floor office the Triumph works in Meriden, Conve try. It is not a big room. In one corne stands a drawing board, in another, bookcase. Spread around are bits ar pieces of engines — Triumph engines. C the outside the door is labeled simp "D. L. Hele."

That is the name behind the success Triumph machines at Daytona, it is t name of the 47-year-old Englishman wh spent his time there with stop watch ar pencil noting everything about six Triump machines and quite a few things abo the opposition. To those on the spot may have seemed uncommunicative, tiring or shy, but the simple answer Doug Hele went to Daytona as archite for a Triumph victory.

Success has to be built on a fir foundation of both theoretical and pra tical knowledge. This is where Doug He scores over so many other developme engineers, for he covers around 10,0 miles a year on bikes, in particular, tho with a problem to be solved. He w apprenticed for five years to the Briti Motor Corporation in machine tool desi and the drawing office and worked wi them as a draftsman until 1945. Sin Doug could not get onto the design sid he joined the now defunct Douglas co cern and did the original sketch of t radiadraulic fork and worked on its cor ponents, but had nothing much to do wi the engines, which he was really after.

At that time, it was his ambition join Norton on the design and develo ment side, and he achieved this in 194 working with Joe Craig and Bert Ho wood. Then Hopwood went to BSA, ar in 1949, he asked Hele to join BSA design and build a 250cc racer. This itself could well be the subject of anoth article; suffice it to say at this stage th two years were spent on a completely ne design, not only the single cylinder oh four-valve, twin-carburetor engine with ou side flywheel, but also the frame and su pension. It was built in 1951 and after couple of years development, produced most 30 bhp. With Geoff Duke on boa it equalled the Oulton Park class la re

22

The nucleus of Triumph success: Jack Shemans, Arthur Jakeman, Hele and Les Williams.

rd in secret tests, but a directional requirement before racing of a guarantee to win meant the project was shelved. A look of "99 percent perspiration" appears as Doug recalls that particular decision.

In 1956, he went back to Norton with a free hand as development engineer on the Manx models. There, he had a great deal to do with the design of the Jubilee. At that time, the 500 and 650 Dominators, which Hopwood had designed back in 1947, were not very quick; the Manx engine was giving bevel trouble, which he immediately cured by using the design that appeared in his 250cc BSA. Hele learned a lot during 1957 and '58 from engines left by Joe Craig, not the least being that bhp is just as necessary at 5,400 at it is at 7,400. In 1957 he started development on the 500cc Dominator twin, using Manx type cams with a ramp, and by 1961, had the engine turning out 52 bhp with very good torque from 5800 to 7400 rpm. That year, Phil Read was set to ride it in the Senior TT, but fell off in practice, and Tom Phillis rode instead. Nineteen-inch wheels were used and half a link had to be added to the chain to gain sufficient clearance; but even so, the tire touched the frame at the bottom of Bray Hill and smoke can just be detected in the photo of Phillis at that spot during his memorable 100 mph lap. That, done in 1961, is still the only twin and only push rod engine to have lapped the island at over the "ton."

This was a peak period of development at Norton, for that year, in the Thousand Kilometer race at Silverstone, they took the 350, 500 and 650 classes. Speed for the 650 had been obtained by a head Doug redesigned in 1957, to allow Amal GP carburetors. Then, in 1962, the Yanks had a yearning for 750s, so the 650 was bored out to 73mm to accommodate the taste.

Meanwhile, other work had been going on, namely a desmodromic idea Doug had worked out before going to Norton, and Bob McIntyre practiced on it on the final TT practice morning of 1960, but it didn't have the torque of a conventional Manx. A 350cc desmo in 1961 lacked a good compression ratio. A 500 top on a 350 was tried but not raced. The difficulty was to get accurate cams for the desmo. Also, it broke vertical shafts and this led to an improved design for the Manx engine. In an attempt to shorten the stroke, a 93mm bore engine was tried. However, it required a narrower valve angle, so it was dropped.

Then, in 1962 came the move south to London, so that all could be under the AMC roof at Plumstead. Doug Hele toyed with the idea of joining the Ford Motor Company or teaching technical drawing, which he had previously done part time. However, motorcycle engines were his life, and late in 1962, Doug joined Triumph,

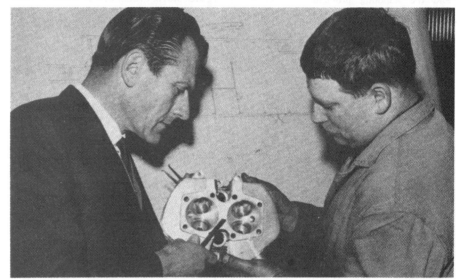

Doug Hele with Ron Barrett, who did all the cylinder head work on the Daytona machines.

Tom Phillis, Domiracer, 1961 Senior TT. The only twin to lap the Island at over 100 mph.

in charge of development where he renewed his association with Bert Hopwood.

The first problem Doug tackled was cam wear on the unit construction 650, which was already a good motorcycle as a result of design work by Brian Jones and development by Frank Baker. Doug overcame the problem by using bigger

TRIUMPH GEARBOXES

BY PATRICK F. OWENS, JR.

cams, while at the same time employing barrel type push rods to cut out side whip. Power was very good on open megaphones, so to get the same with mufflers, a balance pipe and 1¼-inch pipes instead of 1½-inch were used with special silencers.

Doug did not ride in his first few months at Triumph, but when he did, he fully understood the problem facing Percy Tait, the development rider who raced the machines. To cure the handling misdemeanors, he felt that more trail with the existing wheelbase was required. This was achieved by taking 0.775 inch out of the top tube and altering the head angle. This also gave a lower center of gravity. Then, for racing in 1964, the top yoke was altered slightly, fork movement lengthened, and the handling problem was solved. The back end had not been touched, apart from the rate of dampening.

In September, 1965, it was decided to race at Daytona in 1966, so Rod Coates and Cliff Guild went to Meriden to give the lowdown on the American scene. It was notebook, stop watches and coats off in 1965, for they had their problems in practice from which a lot was learned. But it was worthwhile — Buddy Elmore won.

"We learned from each other on that trip," says Doug, "not the least being the use of hard-faced cams which Cliff Guild had been using. It pays to have the same size cams at the end of the race as you start with."

The story of the 1967 races is told elsewhere, but it is worth noting that Triumph went to Daytona with 18-inch wheels which were not too popular. A change at the back to 19 saw three seconds knocked off lap times in practice.

"You cannot argue that 18-inch wheels should be all right when a rider can give that sort of answer," says Hele. When asked if any down-field runner had impressed him, he opted for Gene Romero, whose machine was not really right in practice and possibly did not get all the attention it deserved. But the bike was put right by race time and Doug is pretty sure he'll be among the leaders in 1968.

That brings us to next year, when Doug hopes Triumph will go back to try for three in a row.

"By then we will need more power to pull a higher gear, assuming Harley does some work in the meantime," claims Hele. "Rockers, cams, combustion chambers are the avenues of approach, and we shall also redesign the exhaust mounts, particularly at the engine end."

It will be a diligent search for more power, as Doug Hele is a chartered engineer who expended a lot of perspiration getting his A.M.I. Mech. E. (Associate Member of the Institute of Mechanical Engineers).

Squish heads and all that? A brief grin appeared on Doug's face as he countered, "The Domiracer did not need that in 1961."

You can bet your life the old saying is wrong. There will be more than 1 percent inspiration from this man before practice starts for Daytona in 1968. ∎

Patrick Owens can be found, most of the time, in the competition shop of Johnson Motors' service department. Pat is regarded in the trade as one of the top builders of Triumph TT machinery in the country (just ask Eddie Mulder), and this isn't hard to understand when we discover just how thorough Pat is with his preparation of racing equipment. The piece that follows is typical of the items in Pat's bag of tricks, and while the specific points of modification deal with a Triumph 650 gearbox, they could very easily be applied to transmissions of several different makes.

THE MOTORCYCLE GEARBOX is probably the most highly stressed component of the entire machine, and this is certainly true in the cases where 650cc Triumph engines are reworked for greater horsepower. In most cases these motorcycles are raced on irregular dirt surfaces where the machines frequently became airborne and land with the throttle on. This impact can only be absorbed after the stresses have transferred back through the chain, gearbox, and into the clutch hub rebound rubbers. Unless this happens in fourth gear, the impact drives back through four separate gears in the gearbox.

Lubricant in the gearbox does have a great effect on the life of these gears. With unit construction, engine heat is transferred into the gearbox, thus affecting the viscosity of the lubricant. After experimenting with several different kinds and quantities of oil, the following was found to give the best results: A full quart of Gulf Automotive Hypoid gear lube, or a pint of STP and a pint of SAE 50 weight under extremely hot conditions, like cross-country desert racing.

This greater quantity of oil will give better lubrication especially to the mainshaft and the gears on this shaft, which are located above the gearbox layshaft.

Venting the gearbox to atmosphere will eliminate build-up of internal pressure when the oil becomes heated. With no internal pressure, there will be very little oil seepage from either the kickstarter shaft or the gearshift levershaft, even with

New indexing plunger assembly (left) has been fitted with a heftier spring (T-1604) and has had a drilled nut welded to the spring dome. In conjunction with the drilled drain plug, this vital component can now be secured with safety wire.

he increased quantity of oil.

Shifting under racing conditions is always critical, and missing a shift has made the difference between winning and finishing second in some races. Lightening the camplate in a Triumph gearbox greatly reduces the chances of missing a shift. In most instances when a shift is missed, the gearbox actually shifts by the gear being engaged. The rotating weight of the camplate has a certain amount of flywheel action. This inertia effect is greatly reduced by reducing the weight of the camplate itself. In addition to lightening, fill-welding the neutral notches between second and third and between third and fourth on the camplate is recommended to reduce the possibility of selecting one of these unwanted neutrals. Caution should be taken to make sure the neutral notch is retained between low and second for starting and warm up to eliminate a possible accident if the positive neutral was not retained between these two gears.

The indexing plunger and spring which stops the camplate should be inspected closely when working on the gearbox. The replacement high-tension spring, T-1604, should be used in conjunction with the other modifications.

The drain plug on the Triumph gearbox has a steel tubing extension which is used as a level checking device. It is good practice to braze this permanently to the drain plug itself. The higher level will be above the pipe when using the full quart of lubricant, but this will eliminate the chance of it coming adrift. Also, welding a drilled nut to the plunger spring dome nut provides a safety wire attach point, and drilling the drain plug will allow these two to be safely wired together.

Last, but most important of all, the gear shift lever should be secured to the gearbox. In addition to the standard clamping bolt, drilling a small hole through the lever and shaft for safety wiring provides a positive safety. Drilling the head of the lever clamping bolt for safety wiring gives a double safety and will solve the problem which affects most riders and tuners at one time during their careers. ∎

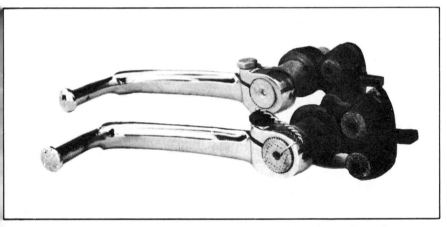

Race-ready gear selector (foreground) has been drilled so that safety wire passes through selector arm and shaft, and then, as a double safety, passes through the head of the clamping bolt.

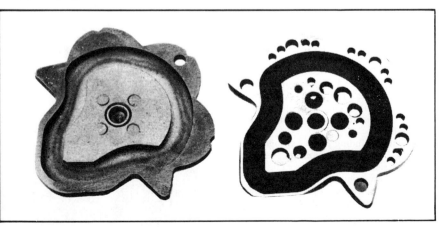

Lightened camplate (right) weighs cosiderably less than standard item. Note absence of second-to-third and third-to-fourth neutral notches.

500 TRIUMPH METISSE PLAYBIKE

OH NO, ANOTHER METISSE in the pages of CYCLE WORLD ! This one's the Mk IV Metisse frame, inhabited by a near-stock 500cc Triumph engine. The Mk IV frame is the next logical step from the IIIA motocross frame. Intended primarily for smaller modern 500-class engines such as the Triumph twin or the BSA 441 single, the new frame boasts several improvements over the old one, some of them with the American rider in mind.

Structurally, the most important change has to do with the top tube cluster; the bottom pair of tubes in this group now run from the steering head back in a continuous arc to the swinging arm pivot assembly, affording the strength advantages of an unbroken, unwelded, sweep of tubing between these two highly stressed points. Obviously, the model change has been made with strength and rigidity in mind as the Mk IV weighs only 1/2 pound less than the Mk IIIA.

Oil is still carried in the frame but the filler plug has been moved from its former position at the back of the steering head to the point where the upper pair of top tubes articulates into the rear subframe section. It remains exposed between the fuel tank and the molded-in seat. This eliminates three problems. Before, it was difficult to tell how much oil there was in the frame unless it was completely topped up. Rear-set bars made filling difficult, too. More important, there was no provision for frothing. With the new filler location, the upper top tubes, being higher than the filler hole, remain empty and the lubricant is routed in such a way that the tubes now serve as a froth tower. Oil ca-

pacity is three quarts, plus whatever is in the engine.

Mark IV owners will find that the engine goes in easier than on the old model; instead of being like a tangle puzzle, the task may be accomplished from either side and the engine plates may be installed after the powerplant is in place.

The rider sits 1 inch lower on the Mk IV and his footpegs are 1-1/2 inches rearward as well as being an inch lower. Word comes from the Rickmans through USA importer John Steen that folding footrests will be optional, although the rigid type were mounted on our test bike.

Welcome to trail riders and competitors in long distance events will be the export model three-gallon gas tank, an alternate choice to the old two-gallon tank. Styling of the big tank is excellent. We understand the Rickmans sent it back to the drawing board three times before they got it "right." The fiberglass finish seems excellent, and the glass itself is more rigid due to the stronger box shape incorporated in the tail piece. The color was a beautiful medium-dark blue, and Steen has inveigled the Rickmans into calling it U. S. Racing Blue.

The kit—including frame, swinging arm, seat and fiberglass components — sells for $695 stateside.

The other goodies on this particular Mk IV were selected by the new owner, Steen P-R Director Lynn Wineland. They include an Airheart go-kart disc brake at the rear and an MZ brake hub assembly at the front. The rear wheel hub is reversible should the rider need to even out tire wear; it consists of the splined halves of

two BSA Gold Star hubs welded together.

An 18-inch front wheel was chosen so that the rider could mount a size 4.00 tire and still have a reasonably light front end. This seems to us to produce a slight tendency to dive over jumps rather than the desirable bit of front end aviation that one normally expects from the Metisse. This is only natural as the frame was designed with a 21-inch front wheel in mind. The difference is cancelled out somewhat, as the Ceriani forks that come over here are somewhat longer than those sold to Continental motocrossmen. Wheel size and tire profile and thickness are personal things though, and where one man prefers to steer the front the other is happier to skate it. Those who follow the example here will get a good ride in the sand, but better be prepared to counter front end skate with lots of throttle twitch on the harder stuff.

There are some other terrific little details that go into making this a very sophisticated play bike. The rear hub carries four sealed ball bearings, two for the wheel, one for the sprocket and one for the brake disc. Timken tapered roller bearings carry the fork assembly in the steering head. All nuts and bolts are high tensile alloy. The horseshoe sparkplug guards came about when one of the Rickman brothers knocked a plug off with his knee while leading in the last lap of a scrambles, thereby losing a $2,800 purse.

The handlebars, believe it or not, are Rickman-designed for export.

All the detail efforts resulted in a weight of 291 pounds ready to run with a full three-gallon tank of gas. This may not seem impressive for a 500cc Triumph-Metisse until one takes note that this is a fully rigged desert sled.

TRIUMPH® '68
The Ultimate in Motorcycling

TRIU

presents t

*Tr

28

It's here. The swingingest, scorchingest group of motorcycles ever assembled under one roof. Triumph for 1968. Unbeatable . . . and definitely available at your Triumph dealer's! New excitement. New power. The ultimate experience on two wheels. So put away your old ideas about what a motorcycle is made to do. And reach for the big ride for '68 on Triumph's new Action Line.

MPH®
Action Line for '68

ds the A.M.A. approved World's Speed Record, e, Utah, 245.667 m.p.h. (with streamlined shell).

TR6C Trophy Special
Single Carburetor / 650 c.c. (40 cu.in.)

Winner of more cross country events than any machine you can name. Called the "Desert Bike." Color: New Hi-Fi Riviera Blue. Polished stainless steel fenders.

T100R Daytona Super Sports
Twin Carburetors / 500 c.c. (30.5 cu.in.)

This is it. The bike that sent all past Daytona records into oblivion. Color: New two-tone Hi-Fi Aquamarine and Silver.

T120R Bonneville
Twin Carburetors / 650 c.c. (40 cu.in.)

What else is there to say? Bonneville. Owns the world record for speed* . . . and that's just the beginning. Color: New Hi-Fi Scarlet, with polished stainless steel fenders.

T100C Tiger Competition
Single Carburetor / 500 c.c. (30.5 cu.in.)

The Tiger doubles up for '68 with new road features to add to the excitement. Color: New Hi-Fi Aquamarine. Polished stainless steel fenders.

TR6R Trophy Sports
Single Carburetor / 650 c.c. (40 cu.in.)

Has the guts to outlast every machine on the road today. Color: New two-tone Hi-Fi Riviera Blue and Silver.

TR25W Trophy 250
250 c.c. Lightweight

Completely new for '68. Handles with cat-like ease on road and trail alike. 4 cycle OHV, single cylinder. Color: New Hi-Fi Scarlet.

29

THROUGHOUT THEIR RECENT HISTORY, commencing about the time they started to seriously export their motorcycles to this country, Triumph's line included a model that seemed to be, in every way, something just for the American buyer. The model was the Thunderbird, christened long before Ford Motor Company's personal car was ever conceived. Almost from the moment the model was announced, it was the thing to have, to aspire to. Its initial appeal was its performance; with the exception of the tempermental hinged-in-the-middle Vincent V-twins, the Thunderbird was about the fastest thing on the road. For several years, the T-Bird held its own, and built up a following of enthusiasts who wanted a fast, comfortable roadburner that was manageable in city traffic, and had some life left in it when all of the zeros on the odometer had been replaced with positive digits.

In the late 1950s, it became apparent to Triumph that everyone had seen all their white rabbits; the time was ripe for a new line-leading big roadster, with more suds than the standard-bearing Thunderbird offered. The new 40 incher was called the Bonneville — its name, too, hinted at the market for which it was destined. Triumph chose, wisely, to continue offering the Thunderbird, for by this time, its following was so great that its cancellation would surely have cost the company sales.

The Bonneville, like the Thunderbird, proved very successful — so much so, that the 'Bird lost its grasp as the emphasis on performance continued to grow, and the "Bonnie" grew with it. Then, the Triumph line for 1967

TRIUMPH 650 SAINT

Sainthood for the Thunderbird

was announced and, as we have all come to expect each year, there were numerous meaningful improvements to be enjoyed. But the most startling thing about the new catalog was the absence of the Thunderbird: the old dear had been, after all, phased out. In the main, the 'Bird's no-show met with reasonable acceptance because it could be rationalized that it had been replaced with the slightly quicker TR6R model, which had proven itself for several years in the lineup, and, to all but the most careful observers, this would pass for the retired 'Bird. Perhaps it was out of reverence for the model, or perhaps it was because of the stigma that the scooter-like rear shroud and old-fashioned headlight nacelle brought to it in its last couple of years, but whatever, Triumph elected to drop the Thunderbird name from its rolls altogether.

And now you're probably expecting us to announce that after a year's sabbatical, the Thunderbird will return to the Triumph line next year. Sorry, but as far as we know the 'Bird is dead and gone for all time. However, Triumph is about to start marketing a model in this country that's as much a Thunderbird as any unit to bear the name. The name of the replacement is the Saint — not nearly so thrilling or imaginative as Thunderbird, is it? Trust us; it is a Thunderbird.

Before you start dancing about, shouting, "Look what Triumph's just done for us!" we'd better explain about the Saint. It's not a new model; fact of the matter is, it's an old model — almost as old as the Thunderbird. You see, it's a . . . uh . . . er how should we say it . . . it's a Triumph police bike. Are you ready for that? Not all of the minions ride 74s. In almost all other parts of the known world, peace officers exit from their houses each morning

and throw a leg over a 40-inch Triumph! For law enforcement work, the Saint, with its relatively light weight, spirited performance, easy starting, cool running and high degree of reliability, has proved popular.

It's no secret that several European and a couple of Japanese motorcycle manufacturers have been trying to gain acceptance for their police models in the U. S., but their efforts thus far have been fruitless. For reasons best known to them, Triumph has not been concerned about not being able to crack this lucrative market, and instead, has decided to make the bike generally available in the U. S. If a three-bike police force in a small mid-west city wants to try Saints for a time, well and good, but in the meantime, if a fireman in Schenectady wants a well-mannered, strong twin for transportation, he too may purchase a Saint.

The chief characteristics that make the Saint so good for police work — soft tune wth lots of cubic inches — also make it a good touring and transportation bike for the man who is faced with more than just a few miles each day. Compression ratio and cam timing are mild, and as a result, starting is child's play, and the operating noise level is noticeably low, with the legion of little mechanical sounds that attend the running of a big twin almost inaudible. Internal engine geometry is complemented by the small (1⅛-inch) Amal Monobloc, with a handlebar-mounted choke control. The Saint is perfectly content to creep along at just-balancing speed in heavy traffic, and it takes only a few miles of this type of running before one discovers that the throttle does not have to be continuously blipped to keep the engine clean; simply let it idle along much as you would the family car.

The small choke size also simplifies the starting drill in that the engine prefers to be a tad wet, cold or hot. Open the fuel cocks, close the choke, crack the throttle and kick it through, and a one-prod start is assured each time.

The Saint's frame is the standard item found on any of the current Triumph 650s, a single loop type with sturdy forgings used for the major junctions. To the devotee of the super-triangulated, double-loop all-welded skeleton, the Triumph component looks like something you'd encourage your mother-in-law to hot-lap with on the Isle of Man. The appearance is deceptive; the Saint, like other recent Triumphs we've tested, is a stable handler, devoid of pitching and yawing, even when bent hard into bumpy turns. In addition to being extra stout, the frame employs two other features that aid its stability: head angle is shallow, contributing to high-speed stability; and the hefty swing arm is pivoted at four points with the outer two located at the extreme frame width, and as a result, the rear end absolutely refuses to flex. Suspension is typical of what we've come to expect of the marque in recent years. The rear spring-shocks are the ubiquitous and always excellent Girlings. The front forks are, of course, Triumph's own, and must qualify as some of the best production units available. Compression and rebound damping cannot be faulted, and the pinch bolts on the base bridge and the two cinch bolts on each axle cap keep the legs in accurate and constant relationship, even under severe sideloading.

The Saint's brakes, like its suspension, are characteristic of Triumph's offerings in recent years and are predictably good. The rear stopper is a no-frills, cast iron type, with a single-leading-shoe arrangement that is rod actuated. For anything short of panic stops, it will pull the motorcycle down swiftly and comfortably, and it takes more than a few repeated stops before fade can be detected. The front unit is also cast iron, housed, in this case, within a full-width hub. Although it is unvented, it handles heat well, owing in part to being cast iron, and handles its chores confidently and smoothly without a trace of shudder. With regard to the sophisticated brakes that are currently available on many touring bikes, the Triumph units are a bit old-hat; however, their excellent performance cannot be disregarded, and for anything short of all-out racing, they are uncommonly good.

Rider comfort is a major consideration for the Saint, and not surprisingly so when it is considered that the bike is intended to be ridden every day for a full work shift. The strange looking half-seat becomes even stranger in appearance with its short ridge across the back, but one must "sit" the bike for a couple of hours before the design can be appreciated. As a solo saddle, it's the best. As with a well-designed automobile bucket seat, the Saint's platform keeps the rider sitting erect so that the spine, and not the fatigable muscles, carries the bulk of the load of the upper body. The rear ridge prevents the hips from rolling back, and consequently keeps the spine

from bowing. We'll give odds that Triumph enlisted some outside aid in designing this orthopedic device. And we thought that their new twinseat was good! It goes without saying, though, that the Saint is not outfitted for a passenger. A pillion pad could be added to provide minimal comfort to a second occupant for short distances, and a set of pillion pegs are fitted to the bike, but we would strongly advise against an invitation being extended to anyone one does not wish to discourage from the sport. For the loner who would fit a luggage rack for campout touring, or for the commuter who fits one to which he can secure a briefcase, the Saint's arrangement is good, providing all sorts of room on which to place things. But for the girl you're about to propose to . . ! If two-up comfort is essential, it will be necessary to purchase a Triumph twinseat and slip it on in place of the solo model — they use the same attachment scheme of hinges and pull lock.

The handlebars and foot controls coordinate nicely with the seat to keep the rider upright and forever comfortable. Both the hand and the foot controls require reasonable amounts of pressure, and at no time does manipulation come close to being a chore. The bars fitted to the Saint are a wide, moderately pulled back pair that are carried in a rubber-mounted pair of short risers. When maneuvering the bike in and out of the garage, they feel as though they are not attached to anything in particular. Underway, they are another matter, feeling as positive as if they were rigidly mounted, but without acting as a transmission medium for engine and road vibrations.

The Saint's electrics are better than good, and the headlamp beam leaps well down the road ahead of the bike. The automotive type paired horns are the strongest we've seen — or heard — on any motorcycle, and what a pleasure it is to ride a motorcycle with a voice that will urge sleepy-brained motorists back into their own freeway lanes. We strongly hope that some accessory distributor in this country will offer these one day soon, for they are not only stout, but each unit is the size of the regular "peep-peep" type horn that is found on most road bikes.

The Saint's finish is excellent. Welds are clean, castings are superb, polish is lustrous, chrome is brilliant and paint is without flaw. The paint is probably the most outstanding physical feature of the motorcycle — unmarred, untrimmed white on tank and fenders. In the telling, this might not seem to be so much, but in the flesh, it becomes startling.

At first encounter, with its odd looking seat, one knows instinctively that there is something different about the Saint. As we rode it about the city, we were regarded with suspicious stares from other motorcyclists; and ticket-writing highway patrolmen would momentarily forget their business and gape longingly as the Saint whispered by, its rider sitting erect and refreshed.

Triumph broke some hearts when they discontinued the Thunderbird, but they're going to patch those up and win a few more in the bargain with their Saint. ■

TRIUMPH 650 SAINT

SPECIFICATIONS

List Price	$1299
Suspension, front	telescopic fork
Suspension, rear	swing arm
Tire, front	3.25-19
Tire, rear	3.50-18
Brake, front	8 x 1.63
Brake, rear	7 x 1.2
Total brake swept area, sq.-in.	67.3
Brake loading (test weight/swept area)	
lb/sq.-in.	8.1
Engine type	ohv vertical twin
Bore and stroke	
(inches-millimeters)	2.79 x 3.23, 71 x 82
Displacement (inches^3-centimeters^3)	39.6, 649
Compression ratio	7.5
Carburetion	1-1/8" Amal Monobloc
Ignition	battery and coil
Bhp @ rpm	40 @ 6500
Oil System	dry sump
Oil capacity, pts.	6.0
Fuel capacity, gal.	6.3
Starting system	kick, folding crank
Lighting system	generator and battery (2, 6V)
Air filtration	washable gauze
Clutch	multi-disc, wet plate
Primary drive	duplex chain
Final drive	single-row chain
Gear ratios, overall:1	
5th	none
4th	5.11
3rd	6.08
2nd	8.64
1st	12.51
Wheelbase	56.5
Seat height	31.3
Seat width	10.8
Foot-peg height	12.0
Ground clearance	7.0
Curb weight (w/half-tank fuel)	385
Test weight (fuel and rider)	545

PERFORMANCE

Top speed	95
Maximum speed in gears (@ 7000 rpm)	
5th	none
4th	102
3rd	86
2nd	60
1st	42
Mph per 1000 rpm, top gear	14.6
Speedometer error	
30 mph indicated, actually	29.9
50	49.3
70	68.6
ACCELERATION, ZERO TO —	
30 mph, sec.	2.7
40	3.7
50	5.3
60	6.6
70	9.5
80	12.8
90	19.0
100	
Standing 1/8-mile, sec.	9.5
terminal speed	70
Standing 1/4-mile, sec.	15.4
terminal speed	85

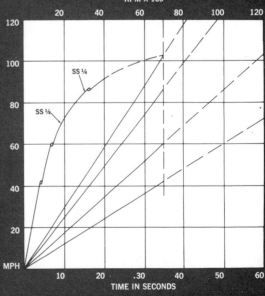

ACCELERATION AND ENGINE / ROAD SPEED
RPM X 100

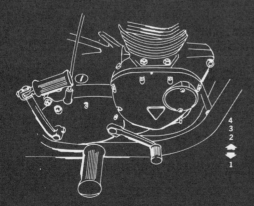

CHENEY-TRIUMPH

BY BRYAN KENNEY

A 242-Lb. Happening For a Familiar Engine

SOMETHING GOOD has happened to the Triumph engine. In the past it probably has been used for more purposes than any other motorcycle powerplant, but it has at last found its way into an Eric Cheney frame. This means something special for the Triumph Twin enthusiast, for it now is the engine of a machine that weighs less than a CZ, that delivers more horses, and yet maintains those three abilities—flexibility, availability and dependability—for which it is so popular.

A sample version, which belongs to Ken Heanes, weighed 242 lb. straight out of the oven with the latest 500 Triumph engine. To make it lighter, the Dunlop tires would have to be exchanged for Barums, and an alloy rim would have to be laced on the front. Then it would weigh just about 235 lb. as a complete bike. Beyond that, holes would have to be drilled in the engine itself, for Eric Cheney has done everything else.

The power-to-weight ratio is startling. It is what could be achieved if the entire engine were taken out of a production 500—and the horsepower were somehow left in. In order to achieve this result, it was not a matter of a week spent on the frame with the drill and file, but one of years at the drawing board developing and redesigning production scramblers for grand prix motocross. Cheney says infinitely more is gained by chopping the weight 30 percent than is achieved by adding 30 percent more horsepower. It works to the motorcycle's benefit in more ways than one. Less weight does not do the single job of increasing acceleration; it also makes the machine stop more quickly, change direction faster, and permits the rider to hang on to the bike with less effort. At a given speed over rough terrain, a lightened machine tends to ride on the tops of bumps, instead of sinking into them.

The drawback, of course, is the fact that structural durability is too often the first thing to hit the garage floor when the drill is applied to lighten the bike. On the Cheney-Triumph the pounds were removed a long time before the first prototype took shape. On the drawing board, large details became small details, at which point they were either incorporated, if possible, into a single detail taking over the functions which had been performed by several, or somehow eliminated altogether. Short 0.375-in. bolts thread directly into an 0.25-in. cross section of threaded tubing welded to the frame at the points where the exhaust pipes are secured. In

this way, the threaded cross section of tubing works simultaneously as a super-light lug and a super-light nut. Footrests fabricated of rectangular tubing are attached independently to the frame in a manner that increases their toughness without necessitating a heavy stud running the breadth of the cradle. Engine plates on the Cheney-Triumph have been done away with, except for two 0.312-in. pieces of aluminum alloy at the front of the crankcases. On Ken Heanes' Cheney-Triumph, the foot brake pedal and the footrest on the left side have been incorporated into one unit.

The duplex frame, which weighs only 16 lb., owes its toughness to three main factors—the type of material, the structural dynamics, and the method of welding. Cheney has found the 16 gauge Reynolds 531 tubing (the English equivalent to U.S. 4130) most suitable for a machine weighing between 220 and 280 lb., and insists that the duplex design has the best potential for lightweight strength. For the welding, he uses a gas-flux process which gives a maximum of flow control with a minimum of heat, which, in turn, insures a smooth, clean weld without interrupting the tensile strength of the tubing. With the engine secured in the frame at the front, rear, bottom and top, the geometry amounts to a structure of triangles in every direction. In

this manner, with the engine and frame working together for structural strength, the frame can be built much lighter and stronger than is usually the case.

There is no secret to the way pounds are spared on other components. The seat is covered on an aluminum base, the airbox is of light sheet aluminum welded to precise dimensions to take maximum advantage of the well between the swinging arm pivot and the seat. The number plates, also in light alloy sheet, offer a lightweight means of covering the air cleaner elements on either side of the airbox. The alloy gas tank is considerably lighter than it would be were it fabricated of fiberglass.

To better existing forks, Eric Cheney has turned to Elektron for the forklegs and Reynolds 531 tubing for the upper and lower crowns. The fork tubes and internals are also of his design. The entire assembly weighs 7 lb. less than Cerianis. Hubs are fabricated of Elektron.

Perhaps the happiest aspect of this Cheney-Triumph is the fact that it is being produced in kit form at the Cheney works in the south of England. Aside from the forks, crowns and wheels, everything but the engine is included in the kit. ∎

TT exhaust pipes mount at two points on the frame beneath the engine to provide protection for the cases.

SLIPSTREAM

Gotcha!

Andrew Sewell Photo

TRIUMPH TRIDENT 750

A Swift New Three For the Connisseur

CYCLE WORLD
R O A D   T E S T

TRIUMPH'S SUPER secret, that didn't remain a secret for long, now is open to public view—officially. After two and a half years of development, the factory's 750-cc ohv Three is here. Exotic projects such as the Three are difficult to keep hidden, and indeed, on both sides of the Atlantic, the motorcycling press and many riders in the street long have known of the bike's existence. During open road testing, it frequently has been cloaked in shabby tank and accessories in attempts to disguise its blatantly different engine. Now, the Three—named the Triumph Trident—is in dealers' hands, for everyone to see.

And it's truly a stirring sight. For, the Three is unique. The world over, there is not another three-cylinder roadster motorcycle in production. The Trident could even be the first non-racing Three ever made, a possibility this test will not press; who knows what obscure maker might have produced a short-lived Three during the shifting fortunes of the early motorcycle industry. Not only is the Trident unusual, it also goes very fast. Only days after its delivery from England to the U.S., it recorded a maximum speed of 117.03 mph. Regardless of piston displacement, that's quick for any street machine. More proof of the Trident's abundant horsepower is available in its quarter-mile time of 13.71 sec.

These figures appeared more than satisfactory, until the Triumph men discovered that, in the rush to deliver the bike for test, slightly inaccurate timing on the center cylinder had

not been corrected. This task attended to, a "pro" drag rider mounted the Trident. Bob Ebeling, AHRA record holder on his 650-cc Triumph fueler, was the man, and he set a shattering time of 13.028 sec., and burst the 100-mph barrier with a top end speed of 102.73 mph. The most ardent of big bike admirers will find nothing to fault in the Trident's straight line accelerative performance.

Most of all, however, the Trident is a prestige motorcycle. An awesome number of people will find that third cylinder irresistible. It will mark its owner as surely as if he were to drive a 427-cu. in. hot pink Corvette Sting Ray among the swarming minicars of the Triumph's homeland...well, almost. Single- and twin-cylinder bikes are commonplace, even Fours are offered by more than one manufacturer. But, there is only one Three.

If three cylinders are not sufficient as a showstopper, the Trident's exhaust note should do the job. As more than one test rider commented reverently, "It's the Ariel Square Four reborn." Just like the now-defunct 1000-cc Ariel, a busy,

slightly hoarse burble of sound is emitted from the Triumph's six little exhaust outlets. No one could mistake this music for the harsher pulse of a parallel Twin. And, when the throttle is open, and the Three is hard at work, the cacophony of sound will turn the head of any motorcyclist within hearing range. This is not to say that the Triumph is excessively loud; the attractiveness of its exhaust note lies in its quality, not in its quantity. Few people will disagree that it's the most exciting road motorcycle to be heard today.

But, why did Triumph choose a Three? The number sounds out of balance, without the symmetry of a twin-cylinder machine, or the unity of a Single. Actually, there is no inherent mechanical barrier that prevents a three-cylinder engine from being totally efficient and reliable. Presumably, Triumph could have moved to a four-cylinder layout. But many factors point in favor of a Three. It should be more efficient and powerful than a Twin of comparable size, and turn at higher speeds. Yet its frontal area, and possibly, its weight, should be less than that of a Four. A vital con-

sideration is that an increase in the number of cylinders invariably means higher manufacturing costs. Thus, while a Three will be more expensive than a Twin, it generally will not be as costly as a Four.

A Three also scores heavily in the matter of balance. A twin-cylinder engine with both crankpins set at 360 degrees is vulnerable to problems of crank flexing, as both pistons move in unison. The flexing sometimes is transmitted throughout the motorcycle, and the rider feels it in the form of vibration. One firing stroke occurs per crankshaft revolution.

But the ideal crankshaft design for a Three is a 120-degree configuration, which Triumph has adopted for the Trident. In such a layout, forces created by the moving parts of the engine are canceled out, and the result is considerably smoother operating characteristics.

The Trident engine is an alloy unit that features some of the neatest looking components to be found on English bikes. Not surprisingly, some parts are taken from Triumph's 500- and 650-cc machines. However, the majority of engine pieces are new. The sturdy, forged, one-piece crankshaft rides in an unusual mixture of bearing types, with two plain bearings in the center, a ball bearing on the drive side, and a roller bearing on the timing side. Big end bearings also are plain. Crankpin diameter, at 1.624 in., is identical to that on Triumph's 650-cc models. Main bearing internal diameters are: plain, 1.91 in; ball, 1.25 in.; and roller, 0.98 in.

Twin camshafts are located fairly high in the block, in typical Triumph style, and pushrod tubes run between the cylinders, also in customary style, and are identical in appearance to those used on Twins. Valve diameters are 1.53 in. for the inlet, and 1.31 in. for the exhaust. Duration for both inlet and exhaust camshafts is 271 degrees.

The aluminum alloy cylinder barrels are cast as one unit, as are the heads, while two separate rocker covers are bolted to the heads.

Drive from engine to rear wheel is transmitted by a triplex primary chain running in an oil bath, a Borg and Beck diaphragm spring single-plate dry clutch (similar to automobile units), a four-speed gearbox, and a single-row chain as final drive. Primary chain adjustment is effected by a rubber faced tension blade. A rubber packed shock absorber unit inside the clutch sprocket assists smooth power transmission.

The Trident's engine/gearbox assembly follows modern unit construction design, but in a rather unusual manner. The crankcase casting is in three sections; the center portion extends rearward to include the gearbox, while two outer casings divide vertically from the center section. In addition, there are separate covers for the primary drive, on the left, and for the timing mechanism, on the right. Unfortunately, this design includes four vertical splits across its width, each of them vulnerable to possible oil leaks. Fears about possible leaks proved well founded, for oil exuded in tiny amounts from the cylinder heads and in greater quantities from beneath the crankcase during the test period.

The dry sump lubrication system follows orthodox design, apart from the groovy looking 0.25-pt. capacity oil cooler mounted beneath the nose of the fuel tank. Oil coolers frequently are employed on road racing machinery, but rarely on touring bikes. Obviously, a Three calls for special consideration. Oil is gravity fed from the tank to a geared pump, and passes through a cartridge filter and along drillways to the center main bearings and connecting rod big ends. The pistons, wrist pins, and outer main bearings are splash fed.

A pressure bleed from the center main bearing caps feeds the exhaust and inlet cam followers. After draining back into the crankcase, the lubricant is drawn through the scavenge side of the oil pump, passes to the oil cooler, and then returns to the tank. An oil line between the scavenge pump and the cooler delivers oil to the valve mechanism. Three separate filters are employed—one in the tank, another in the lower rear end of the crankcase, and a third in the crankcase sump.

Gearbox and primary chaincase contain their own separate supplies of oil. Triumph's customary drip feed system lubricates the final drive chain. An easily accessible screw, located just below the oil tank filler cap, allows for adjustment of the rate of delivery to the chain.

Three 27-mm Amal concentric carburetors supply the mixture, after receiving air through a wire mesh and gauze filter element which cannot be cleaned. A small alloy casting is mounted transversely above the carburetors, and each throttle slide is linked to it. Thus, only one throttle cable is needed—a movement of the handlebar grip simultaneously shifts the casting, and all three slides.

Unmistakably Triumph—that's the verdict on the appearance of the powerplant and its satellite components. And why not make the Three look like a Triumph? The factory already possesses a multitude of followers all over the world for its big Twins, so to make the entire range appear similar is a logical step. A dohc Three, for example, just would not possess the Triumph stamp.

On the road, the Trident is very un-Triumphlike, as any Three must be in comparison with Twins. Certainly, a full throttle blast on the Trident, accompanied by that magnificent bellow of sound from three cylinders, is an exotic sensation.

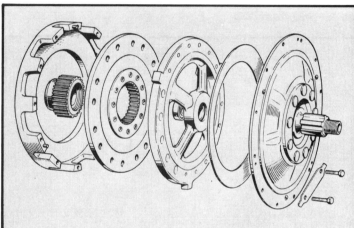

The engine spins quickly and freely to peak rpm of 8000, and is so smooth that it feels more like an automobile unit than a motorcycle engine. This, too, is a characteristic of Ariel Square Fours. Surprisingly, there was little torque at low crankshaft speeds. The engine must turn at 3000 rpm or more before any real degree of low end thrust is felt. Crankshaft design is clearly responsible for at least a part of this effect, for there are two flywheels. The lack of torque, combined with the Trident's weight—almost 500 lb.—makes the bike somewhat of a handful in city traffic. With a passenger on the rear, maneuvering is rather more cumbersome. On the majority of machines over 500 cc, pickup from a halt can be achieved at little over tickover engine speed. On the Trident, particularly two-up, it's a matter of easing rpm to around 3000, and slipping the clutch for a while.

Despite this inconvenience, the bike is definitely a machine for two people to enjoy. The neatly pleated seat is borrowed from the 650 Triumphs, but on the Trident its location appears to have been changed. The rider sits on its immediate forward end, in a natural riding position, and leaves a long expanse of seat for his companion. And, the passenger can lean against, or hold onto, a large grab rail mounted behind the seat. It's one of the best rider/passenger layouts on any motorcycle, and two people could cover many Trident miles without discomfort.

Slight, high frequency vibration *can* be felt, vaguely through the handlebar, more definitely through the footpegs. But the shakes are not excessive, and are no deterrent to ownership of a Trident.

The gear change pedal, mounted on the right as on all British bikes, operates on a one-down, three-up pattern, as on all Triumphs. Swift, quiet upward changes are possible, but down changes require care if a crunch is to be avoided. Clutch lever action is stiff and, when cold, the clutch mechanism drags a little, causing graunches when low gear is selected from rest. Again, this is a Triumph characteristic.

Frankly, the brakes are not up to the task of halting this 500-lb. projectile, in view of the speeds it can achieve. The

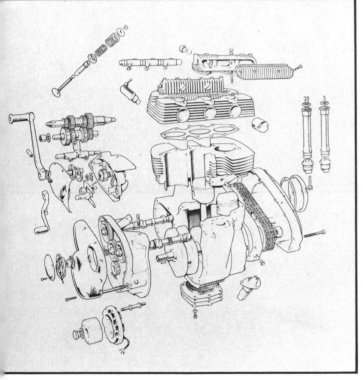

machine for lurid, footpeg-scraping daredeviltry. The bike just does not inspire in its rider that much confidence. The rear tire is Dunlop's new K81 design, a fine cover offering ample grip; the front tire is a Dunlop K70.

For more restrained cornering tactics, however, the Three performs adequately. And as a long distance hauler, it's a keen machine. A rider is likely to arrive at his destination without cramp, and without the numbing effects of vibration. Highway cruising is effortless, and is aided by a softish suspension which absorbs the majority of highway irregularities.

Frame configuration is similar to the layout on 650 Triumphs, except that tubing diameter is greater in some areas. Diameter of the single front downtube has been increased, for example. Two toptubes, one above the other, converge under the fuel tank, and arc downward to a point slightly ahead of the swinging arm pivot. The rear frame legs are bolted to the main frame section, and the swinging arm pivots on bronze bushings.

While the Trident engine is an exciting example of machinery, other aspects of the bike are disappointing. For example, a motorcycle priced at more than $1700 should employ something more refined than fragile strips of rubber to attach horn, dimmer and kill switch electrical leads to the handlebars. These strips, little more than rubber bands, deteriorate rapidly.

The tank is decorated along its top centerline with a strip of hollow plastic that doesn't appear at all durable.

One of the major complaints can be leveled at the exhaust system. Those three little outlets emerging from each silencer would look more at home peeking from beneath the skirts of a motor scooter. The header system consists of a single pipe from each head, with the center pipe dividing into two. One of these center pipes joins the left exhaust tube, the other meets the right one. It's all a kind of a super-siamesed setup. But the area around each of the junctions between pipes very quickly blued, hinting that burnt gases could be momentarily boggling, instead of making a clean exit. The header pipes are bolted to the lower exhaust pipes, with the upper sections fitted outside the joints, forming a possible source of exhaust leaks. Three entirely separate exhaust and silencing systems might have looked sharper, and worked more efficiently.

All early Tridents will be finished in an aquamarine blue color, containing a hint of metalflake finish. The fenders and the 5.12-gal. fuel tank are formed of steel, while fiberglass paneling makes up the bodywork rearward of the seat. A pair of Smiths instruments, a speedometer and tachometer, are fully encased in rubber, and are easily read.

Electrical components include a crankshaft driven alternator, battery, breaker points, and coils. The only variation from convention are a triple contact breaker, and three coils—on the Trident, many things happen in threes! Starting is easy, provided the two outside carburetors are liberally flooded, and twin horns emit a powerful, melodic blare. Powerful lighting takes the difficulty from night riding.

For a final demonstration of the merits of three-cylinder engines, doubters need only look at the history of international road racing. The Italian Guzzi factory, and West Germany's DKW plant, both have constructed successful racing Threes. But perhaps the most famous example of all is the MV Three, which has won the 500-cc world championship for the past three years. In its 350-cc version, it recently clinched the first MV title in that class. So, it appears that Triumph probably will gain indirect publicity from the efforts of a rival factory. But, disregarding racing Threes, there is no doubt that the Triumph Trident is a big, fast, groundshaker of a motorcycle. And there isn't another bike like it. ∎

front brake is Triumph's new twin leading shoe unit, but it is spongy in action, and requires sheer musclepower if the bike has to be hauled down from high speed. Lack of feel is partly because the brake cable is too thin for the duty it has to perform. The tail-mounted brake light is operated from the front stopper—an excellent idea, for any rider with common sense knows that in any stop, the front unit is the one to go for first. Moreover, this feature is expected to become a federal safety standard, which all states will be asked to enforce. The Trident's single leading shoe rear brake just won't do the job it should.

The bike's handling is largely a matter of personal taste, depending on where the rider's prejudices lie. Anyone accustomed to the Olympian agility of Triumph's 650- and 500-cc models, or to a fine handling lightweight, may well find the Three cumbersome and deliberate in comparison. This is particularly true at low speeds. It also is not the most suitable

TRIUMPH TRIDENT 750

SPECIFICATIONS

List price $1765 (p.o.e. west), $1750 (p.o.e. east)
Suspension, front . . . . telescopic fork
Suspension, rear . . . . swinging arm
Tire, front 3.25-19
Tire, rear 4.10-19
Brake, front, diameter x width, in. . . . 8 x 1.625
Brake, rear, diameter x width, in. . . . . . . 7 x 1.2
Total brake swept area, sq. in. 67.19
Brake loading, lb./sq. in. 9.96
Engine, type . . . . four-stroke Three
Bore x stroke, in., cc . . 2.67 x 2.75, 67.0 x 70.0
Piston displacement, cu. in., cc . . . 45.0, 753.0
Compression ratio 9.5:1
Carburetion . . . . . . (3) 27-mm Amal concentric
Ignition . . . . battery, coils
Claimed bhp @ rpm . . . . 60 @ 8000
Oil system . . . . dry sump
Oil capacity, pt. 6.0
Fuel capacity, U.S. gal. 5.12
Recommended fuel . . . . premium
Starting system . . . . kick, folding crank
Lighting system . . . . battery, generator
Air filtration . . . . wire mesh and gauze
Clutch . . . . diaphragm spring, dry
Primary drive . . . . (1.73:1) triplex chain
Final drive . . . . (2.74:1) single-row chain
Gear ratios, overall:1
  5th . . . . none
  4th 4.88
  3rd 5.82
  2nd 8.26
  1st 11.91
Wheelbase, in. 57.5
Seat height, in. 31.7
Seat width, in. 11.5
Handlebar width, in. 27.7
Footpeg height, in. 10.5
Ground clearance, in. 6.1
Curb weight (w/half-tank fuel), lb. 499
Weight bias, front/rear, percent 44/56
Test weight (fuel and rider), lb. 669

TEST CONDITIONS

Air temperature, degrees F 87
Humidity, percent 43
Barometric pressure, in. Hg. 29.94
Altitude above mean sea level, ft. 1632
Wind velocity, mph 9
Strip alignment, relative wind:

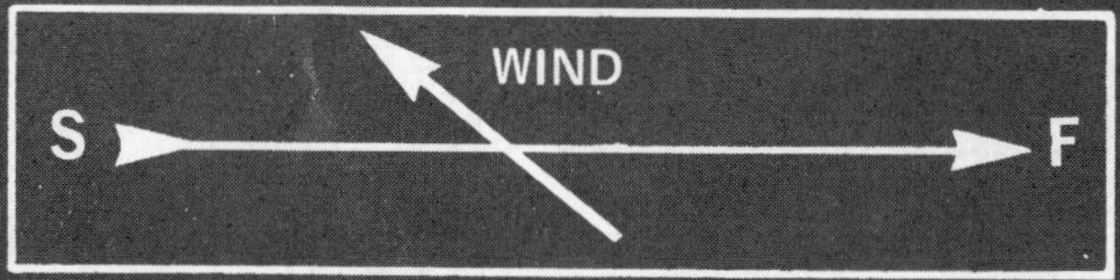

PERFORMANCE

Top speed (actual @ 7452 rpm), mph . . 117.03
Computed top speed in gears (@8000rpm),mph:
  5th . . . . none
  4th 125.7
  3rd 105.4
  2nd 74.2
  1st 51.5
Mph/1000 rpm, top gear 15.71
Engine revolutions/mile, top gear 3821
Piston speed (@ 8000 rpm), ft./min. . . . 3666.75
Fuel consumption, mpg 20.3
Speedometer error:
  50 mph indicated, actually 51.20
  60 mph indicated, actually 62.84
  70 mph indicated, actually 73.95
Braking distance:
  from 30 mph, ft. 36.67
  from 60 mph, ft. 157.0
Acceleration, zero to:
  30 mph, sec. 2.3
  40 mph, sec. 3.1
  50 mph, sec. 4.0
  60 mph, sec. 5.6
  70 mph, sec. 6.7
  80 mph, sec. 8.3
  90 mph, sec. 10.4
  100 mph, sec. 14.3
Standing one-eighth mile, sec. 8.40
  terminal speed, mph 81.44
Standing one-quarter mile, sec. 13.71
  terminal speed, mph 98.46

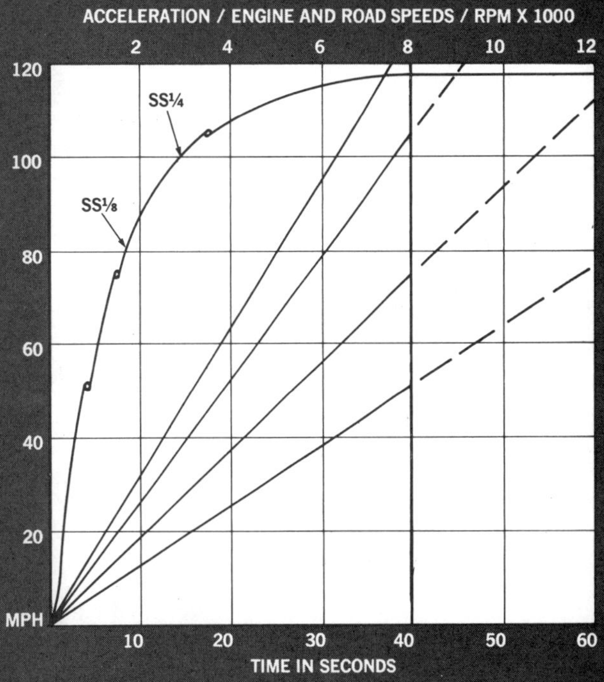

ACCELERATION / ENGINE AND ROAD SPEEDS / RPM X 1000

WIND

S — F

on a '69 Triumph!

Trident Triple T150
Three Cylinder / 750 cc.

The new leader of the pack! Lets you forget about vibrations—at any speed. So powerful we had to develop an entirely new concept in tires to carry it!

Trophy 650 TR6C
Single Carburetor / 650 cc.

Winner of more cross country events than any machine you can name. They named it the "Desert Bike." And you know you got to be rugged and reliable to earn that!

Daytona T100R
Twin Carburetors / 500 cc.

The motorcycle that left all past Daytona records in the dust. Spot it right off by its deep throated growl!

Bonneville T120R

Twin Carburetors/650 cc.

Holder of the A.M.A. approved world's speed record! Of course, it wore a streamlined shell at Bonneville, Utah. But you don't *really* want to go 245.667 mph. Do you?

Trophy 500 T100C

Single Carburetor/500 cc.

Charge it up a mountain, or paw it down the highway. We mated the best features of both a trail and a road bike to come up with this six-time Grand National Enduro Champion.

Tiger 650 TR6R

Single Carburetor/650 cc.

From its sturdy two-piece frame, down to its new 8″ twin-cam front stoppers, the TR6R is probably the most manageable and durable bike ever built.

Trophy 250 TR25W

Single Carburetor/250 cc.

The light fantastic—only 285 lbs., but with big Triumph quality and features. Handles like a cat, on the road or off. The finest 250 cc. motorcycle made.

THE SPECS

MODEL	TRIDENT (T150)	BONNEVILLE (T120R)	TIGER 650 (TR6R)	TROPHY 650 (TR6C)	DAYTONA (T100R)	TROPHY 500 (T100C)	TROPHY 250 (TR25W)
Engine Type	O.H.V.	O.H.V.	O.H.V.	O.H.V.	O.H.V.	O.H.V.	O.H.V.
Number of Cylinders	3	2	2	2	2	2	1
Bore/stroke, mm.	67 x 70	71 x 82	71 x 82	71 x 82	69 x 65.5	69 x 65.5	67 x 70
Bore/stroke, ins.	2.64 x 2.76	2.79 x 3.23	2.79 x 3.23	2.79 x 3.23	2.72 x 2.58	2.72 x 2.58	2.64 x 2.75
Capacity, cu. cms.	747	649	649	649	490	490	250
Capacity, cu. ins.	45	40	40	40	30.5	30.5	15
Compression ratio	9:1	9:1	9:1	9:1	9:1	9:1	10:1
B.H.P. and R.P.M.	60 @ 7,250	52 @ 6,500	45 @ 6,500	45 @ 6,500	41 @ 7,200	38 @ 7,000	22 @ 8,250
Engine sprocket teeth	28	29	29	29	26	26	23
Clutch sprocket teeth	50	58	58	58	58	58	52
Gearbox sprocket teeth	19	19	19	18	18	18	15
Rear sprocket teeth	52	46	46	46	46	46	52
R.P.M. 10 m.p.h. top gear	657	634	634	666	744	744	905
Gear ratios—top	4.89	4.84	4.84	5.11	5.7	5.7	7.82
Gear ratios—third	5.83	5.76	5.76	6.09	6.97	6.97	8.6
Gear ratios—second	8.3	8.17	8.17	8.63	9.16	9.16	11.4
Gear ratios—first	11.95	11.81	11.81	12.46	14.10	14.1	18.3
Carburetor—make	Triple/Amal	Twin/Amal	Amal	Amal	Twin/Amal	Amal	Amal
Carburetor—type	626	930	930	930	626	626	928
Front chain size	3/8" x .225" x .25" Triplex	3/8" x .225" x .25" Duplex	3/8" x .225" x .25" Duplex	3/8" x .225" x .25" Duplex	3/8" x .225" x .25" Duplex	3/8" x .225" x .25" Duplex	3/8" x .225" x .25" Duplex
Rear chain size	5/8" x 3/8"	5/8" x 3/8"	5/8" x 3/8"	5/8" x 3/8"	5/8" x 3/8"	5/8" x 3/8"	5/8" x 1/4"
Tire—front, ins.	3.25 x 19K70	3.25 x 19	3.25 x 19	3.50 x 19	3.25 x 19	3.50 x 19	3.25 x 19
Tire—rear, ins.	4.10 x 19K81	4.00 x 18	4.00 x 18	4.00 x 18	4.00 x 18	4.00 x 18	4.00 x 18
Tire type—front	K 70	K 70	K 70		K 70		K 70
Tire type—rear	K 81	K 70	K 70	Opt. K 70 or Trials Universal	K 70	Opt. K 70 or Trials Universal	K 70
Brake diameter—ins. (cms.)	8F (20.32) 7R (17.78)	8F (20.32) 7R (17.78)	8F (20.32) 7R (17.78)	8F (20.32) 7R (17.78)	8F (20.32) 7R (17.78)	7F (17.78) 7R (17.78)	7F (17.78) 7R (17.78)
Finish	Aquamarine	Olympic Flame/Silver	Trophy Red/Silver	Trophy Red/Silver	Lincoln Green/Silver	Lincoln Green/Silver	Trophy Red
Seat height—ins.	32	30½	30½	30½	30	30	30.
Seat height—cms.	81.3	77.5	77.5	77.5	76.2	76.2	76.2
Wheelbase—ins.	57½	55½	55½	55½	53½	53½	52
Wheelbase—cms.	146	141	141	141	136	136	132
Length—ins.	86¾	84½	84½	84½	83¼	83¼	82
Length—cms.	220.34	214.5	214.5	214.5	211.5	211.5	208
Width—ins.	28½	27	27	27	27	27	28
Width—cms.	72.39	68.5	68.5	68.5	68.5	68.5	71
Clearance—ins.	6½	7⅛	7⅛	7⅛	7⅛	7½	7½
Clearance—cms.	16.5	18.1	18.1	18.1	18.1	19	19
Weight—lbs.	470	386	386	384	354	340	285
Weight—kilos	213.4	175	175	174	161	154	130
Gas—gals.	5.12	2½	3½	2½	2⅜	2⅜	2½
Gas—litres	22.5	11	16	11	10.8	10.8	11
Oil—pints	6	6	6	6	6	6	4
Oil—litres	3.4	3.4	3.4	3.4	3.4	3.4	2.27
Prices (F.O.B. Baltimore, Md.)	$1,750	$1,375	$1,280	$1,270	$1,185	$1,095	$695

OREGON TRAIL

A Triumph Cub Tries The Greatest-Ever Enduro

TEXT AND PHOTOS BY RANDALL A. WAGNER

IT HAD TO BE the greatest enduro ever! It started on the banks of the Missouri River with spring's first thaw, and ended, for those who lived through it, on the Pacific shores during early winter snowstorms. Participants came from all walks of life—farmers, prospectors, members of religious movements, businessmen, housewives, badmen, soldiers and speculators.

For more than 20 years, they annually attempted the one-way trip in four-wheeled, 2-oxpower desert sleds called Conestoga wagons. Entries in a single year's enduro could number as high as 40,000 men, women and children. When it was finally completed, nine graves would line each mile of the route.

The route was called the Oregon Trail. The time was the mid-1800s. In the pages of history, the Oregon Trail is only a footnote, yet it existed long enough to expand America into a land that had been British and Spanish, and civilization to a country that was wild. Along its dusty, rugged path came fur trappers to the Rocky Mountains, emigrant farmers to Oregon, 49ers to California and Mormon Pioneers to the Valley of the Great Salt Lake.

At the summit, where the westbound traveler left Nebraska Territory and entered Oregon Territory, was located the key to the trail, the South Pass through the Rocky Mountains. This was the only place on the continent that offered a wagon road to the northwest. It was a high, windswept plain crossing the continental divide between the snowcapped mountains to the north and the canyonlands of the Green and Colorado Rivers to the south.

Years later, after railroads had made the Oregon Trail obsolete, the country surrounding this Pass for hundreds of miles in each direction was to become a state called Wyoming. That's where I come into the picture. I live there.

I knew of the trail while I was growing up in Lander, and rode in its ruts, from time to time, on horseback, on a delightfully green Cushman Motorscooter, on an equally green Indian Warrior and, finally, on an exceptionally black Matchless. That was in the late 1940s and early 50s. I rode for the fun of riding and knew not where the ruts came from, where they went or who made them. They crossed tough country and offered considerable cycling challenge and, then, that was enough.

Times have changed. Now I'm riding the ruts again, this time on a geared-down Triumph Mountain Cub, from one end of the state to the other. My purpose is now serious, but every bit as enjoyable. My selection of motorcycle transportation was based on practical reasons that fail to limit the fun of riding. But I'll start at the beginning.

Fort Laramie is where 200,000 pioneers set out on the Oregon Trail toward the magic lands of Oregon and California.

About two years ago, the Wyoming Legislature gathered in Cheyenne for one of its every-other-year sessions and accomplished, among other things, the merger of several small state agencies into a new unit of government called the Wyoming Recreation Commission. One of the responsibilities assigned the new agency was the research, development and management of all state historic and archaeological sites.

With such high motives as "a chance to do something new and important for Wyoming" in mind, I left a good photographer's job with the state's Game and Fish Department, and joined the staff of the infant Commission. Director Charles R. Rodermel's instructions were to the point.

"The Oregon Trail is Wyoming's major historic feature," he said. "Few people know what it is. Few people know where it is. Make a movie about it so they will."

Chuck and I had worked together before, and we knew how to communicate. Noting the blank look on my face he added, "See Paul Henerson."

Paul is in his 70s and has spent the better part of those years doing Oregon Trail research—walking the ruts, mapping, reading a vast collection of pioneer diaries, corresponding with people whose grandparents and great grandparents made the trip. He knows as much about it as any man.

He is retired now, having worked on the Burlington Railroad and, later, as Historian for the State of Wyoming. He liked Chuck's idea of an Oregon Trail movie.

"Been trying to get something like that done for 30 years," he said. "You bet I'll help. When do we start?"

It was then the middle of winter, which was the only reason I'd found Paul at home. Whenever the fabled Wyoming wind drops below 30 knots, and the temperature rises above -20 F, he can only be found somewhere along the Trail tracing out another branch.

"This spring," I said. "Soon as it warms up."

Paul figured he could wait until May—that's spring in Wyoming—but no longer. "We'll start at Fort Laramie and end at Fort Bridger," he said. "Have you got a motorcycle?"

The question was a total surprise. "Trail bike," I managed.

"Bring it. It's the only way to really travel the Trail. Don't ride any more myself, but wore out a few when I did."

So it was that early May found us, Conestoga Cub in tow, headed west out of Torrington for the famous old fur traders post known originally as Fort

Paul Henerson examines the Oregon Trail at Mexican Hill. The steep ramp cut by oxen and Conestoga wagons is still apparent.

John, then Fort William and finally, with the advent of the military on the western frontier, Fort Laramie. Before we got there, Paul called a halt, helped unload the Cub and pointed me south.

"Ride a mile or so and see what you find," he said.

What he had in mind was soon evident—even to a rank amateur trail hound. Within the mile of sagebrush prairie I had crossed no less than five distinct parallel sets of trail ruts, untouched since the day they were last used some 100 years ago. I followed the middle set west and soon came to a high bluff overlooking the Fort and the

Laramie River. The other four branches converged with the ruts I had followed making one track.

Excited at my discovery, I stood on the pegs and headed back to report with the Cub roaring, bouncing, jumping and speeding as well as a Cub can roar, bounce, jump and speed.

"I found five sets of ruts that all come together on the bluff over the Fort!" I yelled as the Cub slid to a halt.

"You missed one," said Paul stepping

These wagon ruts in Wyoming sandstone serve as a modern reminder of the pioneer Americans who traveled west. Right is the author's Triumph Mountain Cub.

out of the dust. "A sixth track drops off the bluff north of the others. Look closer next time."

That was my first lesson. Two others followed as we loaded the bike.

"The Oregon Trail is not a single track west," said Paul. "It's really a series of landmarks and campgrounds that the emigrants used to get to their destination. If grass or water became a problem along the main trail, the wagonmaster would lead the train onto one of several branches."

Paul explained that many other factors dictated the route a particular train would use at a particular time, listing such things as weather, the flood stage of rivers, the time of year and the personal preference of different guides.

"There are places where the branches are as much as 20 miles apart," he said.

He also pointed out that Wyoming's low population had done much to preserve the trail ruts. It is one of the Nation's largest states but claims less than 400,000 citizens. The land occupied by the Trail, high, dry bench country mostly, hasn't yet become necessary for human use.

A third important trail lesson came while riding the Cub down the ruts west of Fort Laramie toward Register Cliff. As the ground became increasingly sandy, the ruts grew wider and deeper until they were measured in yards instead of feet. At Register Cliff I asked Paul why.

"Wind erosion," was his easy answer. "The wagon wheels wore off the grass and sage and the wind blew the ruts out. It's still going on."

We spent some time at Register Cliff reading the names of the thousands of emigrants who carved them there in the

1800s. Realizing that days could be spent at the pastime, I kicked the Cub to life and rode on to an area known simply as Oregon Trail Ruts National Historic Site.

Here, near the present town of Guernsey, the trail crossed a low sandstone bench and the 200,000 or so wagons carved a trail that is forever engraved in the rock. In some places the ruts are five feet deep, with wheel marks as sharply defined as if they were made only yesterday. Standing there, waiting for Paul to catch up in the car, I could almost feel the vibration of the wagon wheels under my feet, and hear the shouted demands of the bullwackers and the grunted protests of the oxen.

It was then, on the first day of our trip, that the Oregon Trail became a real thing to me, more than a mark on the ground or a line on a map. I started to understand what had caused Paul to devote most of the leisure hours of his life to it, and the special look in his eyes and the tone of his voice when he spoke of it.

"If you think those are something, you should see the ruts at Mexican Hill," said Paul from behind me. He pointed out a branch of the trail I had missed east of Register Cliff.

Again the Cub roared and jumped and Paul, as usual, was right. These ruts were really something! Again in sandstone and a good deal deeper than my 6-foot-7 was tall. No roads lead to them and few know where they are. They're worth finding!

Headed west once more, I paused to examine the Pioneer's Washtub, a warm freshwater spring that flows 65-degree water today just as it did then. Soon I met Paul at Crazy Tony's in Guernsey, and we loaded the Cub before dinner. It started to rain while we were finishing a great steak, and we called it a day.

The rain continued the next day, cold and with a lingering trace of winter, so a panic call was made to Pete McNiff, our Recreation Specialist in Cheyenne, to bring his pickup—"the one with the mud tires."

Pete arrived by 10 a.m. and I noticed his Trail 90 in the back. "I'll spend a few days," he said. "Somebody has to keep track of you two."

A stone arrow points the older "Big Medicine" trail of the Indians. The Oregon Trail follows "Big Medicine" through the South Pass of the Rocky Mountains.

Devil's Gate, at the east end of the Rattlesnake Mountains, was the pioneer entrance to the Sweetwater Desert beyond.

Actually, the pickup wasn't really needed as the Oregon Trail generally follows the Platte River from Guernsey to Casper, and Highway 26 generally follows the route of the trail. We made good time and took some side trips to examine such outstanding natural trail features as Laramie Peak, the red earth country near Douglas, Natural Bridge and Glen's Rock. Paul pointed out access routes to other trail sites I would visit later when I actually started filming.

In the evening we visited Fort Casper, a well restored trail fort that now sits on the west side of the City of Casper. With about 45,000 citizens, Casper shares "largest in the state" honors with Cheyenne and features such modern conveniences as motorcycle shops. Paul, Pete and I visited several, and I noted Paul eyeing a Greeves Ranger with more than average interest.

The mud tires came in handy the next morning as we traveled southwest on the graded dirt "Oregon Trail Road" past the Avenue of Rocks and Willow Springs. By 9 a.m. the sun was out and the country was drying, and soon Pete and I were on the bikes headed down the trail ruts for Sweetwater Station, Independence Rock and Devil's Gate.

The first of these sites is located at the point where the Trail first hit the Sweetwater River, the waterway that would lead it to, and nearly over, the South Pass. Here was located on Overland Stage and Pony Express station in the days when both shared the Oregon Trail route.

Another few miles in the ruts brought us to Independence Rock, probably the most famous of all Trail landmarks. Paul explained that pioneers traditionally tried to reach this point near the 4th of July and celebrated the event by stuffing black powder in cracks in the rocks surface and setting it off. They also took time to write their names on its granite face and, too often, make use of a nearby pioneer cemetery.

We spent some time riding around, on and over the massive rock before leaving for Devils Gate, five miles beyond. Here the trail approaches then skirts one of the country's outstanding sights. Actually, Devil's Gate is a vertical split in the east end of the rugged granite Rattlesnake Mountains, with sheer sides from summit to river channel. Its sides are hundreds of feet high and so close together it appears that a man could jump across. The river course is so direct that a straight-through view is the traveler's reward.

Devil's Gate marks the start of the Sweetwater Desert, 100 miles long and all under the shadow of Split Rock. Highway 287 cuts a diagonal across it and an occasional ranch or mine road appears, but the Oregon Trail was there first and, for a motorcyclist, is still the best avenue of travel.

We spent a day and a half making the trip, covering ground that few had traveled since the last emigrant wagon rolled west, and seeing the sights that

OREGON TRAIL

The pioneer cemetery at Independence Rock is a reminder that nine graves were dug for every tortuous mile of the Oregon Trail.

Pony Express riders never had time to appreciate. It was for us, as it had been for them, a time of rocky ridges, water crossings, tremendous climbs, steep descents, dry washes, sage, sand, sun and sweat.

Pete's trail ride came to an end in the middle of the desert at a place called Three Crossings. Here the trail and the Sweetwater River squeeze together and intersect three times as both attempt to negotiate a narrow pass through the Sweetwater Rocks. Pete dropped the front wheel of the Trail 90 into a hidden ditch of latter-day origin, and did a swan over the bars. The kink in the 90's front wheel almost matched the kink in Pete's back. Both were eventually fixed in suitable repair shops.

Still, we enjoyed the desert tremendously. More, we agreed, than the pioneers did.

At the end of the desert the Sweetwater River disappears into a deep and barren canyon. The trail follows it in, hesitates, then climbs out over the north rim to encounter Rocky Ridge, a wheel-breaking series of granite outcrops that have the weird appearance of ancient torture devices. To this point,

four-wheel drive vehicles can follow the trail. From here on it's two-wheel country.

Once over Rocky Ridge I paused to look around. Pete and Paul had taken the vehicles around the long way and would meet me at Atlantic City, a mining ghost town some 30 miles distant. To my left was the rim of the beautiful Sweetwater Canyon. To my right was the snow-covered south end of the Wind River Mountains. Ahead, over

Arrival at Independence Rock by July 4 meant the crossing would be completed before autumn snow flurries. Those who were late died.

the reflective surface of the alkaline Lewiston Lakes was the famous South Pass. This, for Trail travelers, was the top of the world.

The Cub was feeling the effects of the 8000-ft. altitude. It was tuned for about 5500 ft., and the added height really showed up in sluggish performance. It was running well, it just seemed a bit relaxed.

I passed the three lakes, noticing a large, stone arrow pointing an older Indian trail and started across rolling, sage-covered country. In each low spot, lingering snow banks leaked water that slowly became rivulets feeding the Sweetwater. The damp soil took on a spongy quality that felt bottomless. I topped a higher hill and saw a small 4-wheel-drive vehicle ahead, and was surprised. I hadn't expected company.

As I rode closer I noticed that the vehicle didn't appear to have any wheels—no, they were there, all right, buried in one of the spongy bogs, right to the frame.

The owner came from behind and waved for help. I rode across the bog, trying to look casual, parked on high ground and walked back. It was a 3-hour job with jacks, rocks, logs and winch. As I said, this is strictly two-wheel country.

At Rock Creek I examined the place where 77 members of Captain James G. Willie's Mormon handcart company met their end in an October blizzard in 1856. A month later another handcart company, led by Captain Edward Martin lost 145 members in a similar storm nearby. That year, 1856, was bad for handcart travel on the Oregon Trail.

I kept a late appointment with Pete and Paul before continuing on through

Willow Creek—gas tank deep but the Cub made it somehow—and to the ninth and last crossing of the Sweetwater at Burnt Ranch. Once across, the trail heads straight west over several miles of flat prairie and crosses a low hill that turns out to be the Continental Divide that separates the waters of the Pacific from those of the Atlantic. From the top it is only a short run to a bubbling display of clear, cold water headed west called Pacific Springs.

Near this point the trail divides into many branches headed for different destinations. The Mormon and Bridger Trails head southwest for Fort Bridger and the Salt Lake Valley. The Sublette Cutoff takes travelers due west for California. Lander's Cutoff heads northwest for Oregon. Sub-branches provide alternate routes and shortcuts.

But, for now, we had traveled far enough to get the feel of the Trail and to wonder at the courage of men and women who crossed it in wagons containing the total of their worldly possessions. They were headed for the unknown in a very real sense. Today's astronauts have, at least, the benefit of exploration by unmanned satelites. The emigrants of the 1800s had none.

Since my initial trip with Paul and Pete, I have spent a great deal of time on the Oregon Trail, riding the Cub, carefully, with the equipment necessary for professional 16-mm motion picture photography in a pack on my back. I have photographed reflections of the rising sun in the Sweetwater River and

This is the barren gorge of Sweetwater Canyon in Wyoming's South Pass—much as it was seen by the pioneers in the 1800s.

the setting sun in the distinctive notch of Split Rock. I have rested and had lunch at the historic pioneer campground under the massive stone arch of Natural Bridge. I have camped on the South Pass, breaking through river ice to get water for morning coffee and riding in 90-degree heat two hours later.

I have traveled the Oregon Trail and all of its major branches as well as is possible 100 years after its last major use. It has been a truly great experience.

Those who'd like to make the trip can drop by Cheyenne. I'll show them the pictures and point—in the right direction—and that's more help than the pioneers got. ◎

ACH BRAND of British machine always has had a definitive model that seems to represent and identify the sum total of a company's production through the years.

Norton is epitomized in its cammer—the Manx. Vincent achieved its zenith with its famous V-twin. The mention of BSA will evoke images, not of its Twins, but of the Gold Star—that venerable 500-cc pushrod Single.

Then there's Triumph's definitive number, the vertical Twin. It's still going strong. The identification, established in racing, came first for Triumph's 500-cc Twin. In 1950, however, the 500 gave way to the 650-cc Thunderbird, a bearish vertical Twin that, while heavy and even more capricious than the 500, overcame the deficiencies of torque delivered by 30 cu. in.

A year before the 650s emerged, in 1949, Triumph had instituted a no racing policy. To introduce the new "Thunderbird" to the public, however, the company elected to perform one nicely concerted bit of racing puffery. The stunt was to take three 650s to Montlhery, the road racing course outside Paris, France, and to run them for one hour, at an average speed just over 100 mph. All three machines were successful.

The 650 Triumph needed nothing else. Overnight, the Thunderbird became the darling of the Ton-Up set. It was big, but neither too big, nor too costly. Its rather curious displacement, hardly oriented to racing class limits, gave it as much, or more, power than a racing Single. Furthermore, the machine was served up with excellent reliability.

Now, almost 20 years later, nothing seems to have changed much. Triumph's 650 still is on the motorcycle market, a little bit better each year, handling sweetened by a robust swinging arm frame and an excellent fork, engine a bit more modern with unit construction, alloy cylinder and head, and, saints be praised, a set of genuine brakes that at last perform the required task. The name Thunderbird has disappeared from Triumph catalogs, to be replaced by Bonneville, Tiger and Trophy.

Both Bonneville and Tiger have a pleasing tautness that separates them from other pushrod Twins. The subject of this report, the Tiger, is an easier bike to get along with, compared

TRIUMPH TIGER 650

To 100 mph, With Love

with the cranky, fidgety-fast Bonneville. The stereotype Bonneville rider is a short-haul sort of guy who slicks his hair back and "gases it" incessantly; he's not out to really enjoy motorcycling, he's out to flog himself and his machine. The rider of the single-carburetored TR6R seems more the person who wants to enjoy his motorcycling, hour after hour, day after day, on a machine that allows itself to be forgotten, yet always remains—in its troublefree brutishness—a memorable bike to ride.

Just for fun, compare the TR6R with the Bonneville. Both are basically the same engine, 649 cc, with bore and stroke of 71 by 82 mm, 9:1 compression ratio, and four-speed, unit construction transmission. The Bonny costs about $90 additional. For that extra moolah, the buyer gets one more carburetor and a hairier cam grind. The Bonny is one of the few production machines capable of producing 100 mph in the standing-start quarter, not to mention a 115-mph-plus speed. But its gas tank holds a full gallon less than the TR6R's tank, which will be irritating to the long distance Bonny rider who will have to stop about every 110 miles. The second carburetor also will be irritating to the rider who likes his idling smooth, and his starting easy.

The Tiger 650 owner cruises 175 to 200 miles on a tank of fuel. His single carburetor nearly always allows the engine to idle properly and start quickly. When he needs to go fast, 100 mph or so is fast enough, and so is a quarter-mile in the 14s and 90s. In short, it takes a real speed freak to shell out cash for those extra numbers.

So what has Triumph done this year to make the Tiger even more attractive to the buyer than it has been? Lots of little things. Like that funny evergreen car from Germany, it looks almost exactly the same as last year's model—but this year it's a bit faster, a bit more reliable, and even a bit quieter.

Inside, the most important thing to happen is the change in piston shape. The piston top, which was wedge shaped, now has a dome configuration with squish area. The result is that the piston is more evenly loaded as the charge fires in the combustion chamber, giving better durability, and possibly less high frequency vibration. Compression, 9:1, is the same. New hardened camshafts and tappets also will prove more durable.

The exhaust tappets, incidentally, receive full-pressure, timed lubrication, a change that was instituted in the 1968 models. O-ring seals in the pushrod covers provide a better seal than the flat rubber washers which they replace.

Externally, two important changes improve the Tiger's smoothness throughout the rpm range and make it phenomenally quiet. The first is the balance tube that links the left and right exhaust headers just after they leave the ports.

Any hot rodder who has been around a raucous straight Six knows why balanced exhaust is used. It works on the vertical Twin because the cylinders fire alternately. With the balance tube, each exhaust phase is absorbed by two mufflers rather than just one, because the exhaust headers are connected. So, the bike runs much quieter. An added bonus from the balance

tube is that low and middle rpm operation is improved, each exhaust benefiting from the extractor action created in the other pipe.

The other change has to do with several improvements to the Amal Concentric carburetor, which was introduced in 1966 and suffered from some minor teething problems. These changes are worth mentioning, not only for the TR6, as they will benefit other machines that use this instrument. An air bleed in the needle valve corrects a tendency for the fuel mixture to go rich just before coming on the main jet. A flat spot that occurred just after going off the idle jet has been corrected by tapering a section of the needle that was parallel in the original Concentric. Fuel pickup position is lower, which will eliminate starvation problems that set in during steep ascents with trials or enduro machines. The new jet holder is longer and places the main jet deeper into the float chamber, with a similar idea in mind. Unfortunately for those who own the old Concentric, these improvements are not interchangeable; an entirely new unit must be bought.

The man to whom the price of a bike comes hard will look askance, should he compare the above improvements, which have evident virtue, with the new oil pressure indicator light and the new front brake light actuation switch, which do not. The oil pressure light, which blesses Triumph's road models, is a "gadget," in the worst sense of the word. At first it seems a good idea. But Triumph Twins already had an oil pressure indicator—a little button which extended itself a half-inch from the right-hand casing when things were okay. The rider could look at it when starting off, or when he came to a stoplight, and most of the time he didn't care much anyway, because oil pressure failure on the Triumph is so rare as to make its continued contemplation, in the form of an idiot light, absurd. Incidentally, the idiot light is actuated by an external pressure-sensitive diaphragm housing that projects from a crankcase outlet near the original button indicator. Nothing has changed really. It just blinks (between 7 and 11 psi) and costs more.

The taillight actuation switch for the front brake is another bit of Mickey Mousery for which Triumph cannot be held responsible. The change was made to conform with U.S. law—the same sort of regulation that so radically affects the auto industry. Operation of the taillight by the front brake as well as the rear brake is redundant; in the majority of riding situations, the rider actuates the rear brake at the same time as the front. How sad it is that the road rider has to pay an extra five bucks for some legislator's undue caution.

To be fair to Triumph, it should be noted the company has made most of the bike's nuts and bolts in American sizes for 1969, which is above and beyond the call of duty. Another

happy change is that the mounting screw in the tachometer drive gearbox is now left-hand, so that cam rotation tends to keep it tight, rather than loosen it. The new front-mounted horn is one of the loudest on any motorcycle. Third gear is slightly lower and closer to second, which improves acceleration from 60 to 90 mph.

It is hard to fault the handling of the big bore Triumph roadsters, as the classic single-loop swinging-arm frame has been refined and strengthened over the years. The Girling rear shocks are—well—they are Girlings, and they work. They appear different only because they have been denuded and ringed with chromed coil springs. The compression/rebound damping fork also is effective, and has sufficient travel to work effectively in the dirt as well as on the road. The only time this generous travel is disconcerting is under hard braking, particularly with the powerful new double leading shoe front brake.

TR6 handling has been an amusing subject of controversy in the British press recently. The defenders are typically loyal owners throughout England who may have owned their Twins for several years. The critics all seem to have one thing in common. They are motorcycle police who must ride the poor TR loaded down with radio and heavy gadget packs at the rear. There are very few bikes made that don't reveal their wobbly worst when subjected to such rear end loading. Such handling problems may be eliminated by reducing the load, or moving it forward to the tank.

The new front brake certainly takes a lot of the squeeze out of stopping. Unfortunately, the drum on the test TR6R seemed a bit out of round, thus a pronounced judder occurred under heavy application. Moreover, the brake had a spongy feel, which made it hard to guess how much braking force was to be obtained from a given amount of hand squeeze. Surprisingly, the new brake does not have a great surplus of stopping power; it is difficult, if not impossible, to make the front tire squeal on high traction pavement. Nonetheless, braking hard at the end of repeated top speed runs was swiftly done, with a feeling of security. The rear brake was beyond criticism.

So there it is—the Tiger that is a little less ferocious to handle, and more pleasing every year, yet still as strong as its name implies. It's a heavy gauge tourer for the rider who wants not brief infatuation, but true love. It will boil sweetly all day at 70 or 80 mph. Its power band is mild and will never require buzzing beyond 7000 rpm. Weighing more than 400 lb., it gives that "secure" feeling, yet it may be thrown around in tight quarters in a graceful sort of way. It is one of the most likely engine sizes to consider for extensive two-up riding, or for hauling a sidecar. It will do the "ton" honestly, yet start first kick every morning. It's an exemplary British bike. ◙

TRIUMPH TIGER 650

SPECIFICATIONS

List price . . . . (f.o.b., p.o.e.)	$1299
Suspension, front . . . . telescopic fork	
Suspension, rear . . . . swinging arm	
Tire, front	3.25-19
Tire, rear	4.00-18
Brake, front, diameter x width, in.	8 x 1.63
Brake, rear, diameter x width, in.	7 x 1.13
Total brake swept area, sq. in.	65.7
Brake loading, lb./sq. in.	8.87
Engine, type . . . . ohv vertical Twin	
Bore x stroke, in., mm . . 2.795 x 3.230, 71 x 82	
Piston displacement, cu. in., cc	40, 649
Compression ratio	9.0:1
Carburetion . . . . . . 23-mm Amal concentric 930	
Ignition . . . . battery and coil	
Claimed bhp @ rpm	45 @ 6500
Oil system . . . . gear pump, dry sump	
Oil capacity, pt.	6
Fuel capacity, U.S. gal.	4
Recommended fuel . . . . premium	
Starting system . . . . kick, folding crank	
Lighting system . 12-V alternator, diode rectifier	
Air filtration . . . . washable element	
Clutch . . . . multi-disc, wet plate	
Primary drive . . . . (2.04) duplex chain	
Final drive . . . . (2.42:1) single-row chain	
Gear ratios, overall:1	
5th . . . . none	
4th	4.84
3rd	6.04
2nd	8.17
1st	11.81
Wheelbase, in.	55.8
Seat height, in.	31.4
Seat width, in.	9.1
Handlebar width, in.	32.7
Footpeg height, in.	10.1
Ground clearance, in.	5.5
Curb weight (w/half-tank fuel), lb.	420
Weight bias, front/rear, percent	46.6/53.4
Test weight (fuel and rider), lb.	575

TEST CONDITIONS

Air temperature, degrees F	52
Humidity, percent	51
Barometric pressure, in. Hg.	30.21
Altitude above mean sea level, ft.	1632
Wind velocity, mph	5-7
Strip alignment, relative wind:	

```
┌─────────────────────────────────┐
│            WIND                 │
│   S ▶ ──────────────────▶ F     │
│              ↙                   │
└─────────────────────────────────┘
```

PERFORMANCE

Top speed (actual @ 6390 rpm), mph . . .	101.35
Computed top speed in gears(@7000rpm),mph:	
5th . . . . none	
4th	112.2
3rd	90.0
2nd	66.5
1st	45.9
Mph/1000 rpm, top gear	16.02
Engine revolutions/mile, top gear	3750
Piston speed (@ 7000 rpm), ft./min.	3770
Fuel consumption, mpg	54.21
Speedometer error:	
50 mph indicated, actually	49.07
60 mph indicated, actually	60.04
70 mph indicated, actually	71.31
Braking distance:	
from 30 mph, ft.	38.92
from 60 mph, ft.	147.83
Acceleration, zero to:	
30 mph, sec.	3.2
40 mph, sec.	4.2
50 mph, sec.	5.7
60 mph, sec.	7.1
70 mph, sec.	9.3
80 mph, sec.	11.6
90 mph, sec.	15.5
100 mph, sec.	24.8
Standing one-eighth mile, sec.	10.13
terminal speed, mph	74.68
Standing one-quarter mile, sec.	14.85
terminal speed, mph	89.28

ACCELERATION / ENGINE AND ROAD SPEEDS / RPM X 1000

DUNSTALL 750 TRIUMPH

It's a Pseudo-Racer For Serious Play,
But Treat the Brake Lever With Care.
and Watch Out for the Law.

CYCLE WORLD
R O A D   T E S T

THERE IS A BREED of motorcyclist endemic to England but increasingly common in the U.S.—the cafe racer. The English cafe racer/enthusiast is a sight to behold. Rather than the lazy ape-hangers and sissy bars of supine highway cruising, his bike sports clip-ons, rear set pegs, and road racing tank and seat suited for prone navigation of the cobblestone. Though uncomfortable, that's where it's at in England and that's why Dunstall can sell something like the 750 Triumph with street equipment.

The Dunstall Triumph is a high-mettled racer/tourer in its own right and is made for experienced and disciplined guidance. It is a serious machine capable of genuine ferocity. Not given to merriment, but to hard challenge, it will slip through the wind at better than 120 mph and rage over the landscape with choleric haste.

It is not the machine for one of marginal experience and more than emotional abandon is needed to ride it well. There's more to racing the Dunstall than sitting astride it and working the levers. This bike is no fun at all under 80 mph unless you like being stared at by the curious. It plainly does not lend itself to about-town ego-feeding cruises and is quite unhappy under 30 mph even in low gear. But if you have lots of room or access to a road race course, the Dunstall is a sheer gas. It also is a hot rod, so one can be a bit more forgiving of the weird noises, oil puking and smoking—things that would be strongly criticized on a more standard production bike. We should mention that these disturbances occurred, however, and the prospective buyer in America would do well to come prepared with Locite, extra screws and wire—and be a halfway competent mechanic.

The Dunstall's handling is excellent. At high and low speeds it behaves exactly the way a bike should; we couldn't ask for more. The 750 is one of the best handling motorcycles ever tested by the CYCLE WORLD staff. This fact is rather amazing because the frame, front forks and rear Girling spring/dampers are T 120 units, a definite tribute to the innately good handling characteristics of a production Triumph. It also demonstrates how much you can improve the handling of any bike by installing clip-ons, moving the foot pegs rearward, and using road racing style tires—especially a ribbed front tread, rather than the usual K-70, which allows the rider to hold a truer line when the bike is leaned over hard. This is particularly evident on the Dunstall, as it can be cranked over so truly to the precise angle of lean that at racing speeds it doesn't feel heavy at all when pushed through a turn—and this is a machine of substantial dimensions. Its ground clearance is generous, thanks to the Dunstall pipes and mufflers, and the bike must be hung out at a precarious angle before things begin to scrub away. The centerstand is vulnerable during low leaning lefts, however. In spite of this, and regardless of the bike's attitude or speed, the rider enjoys a sensation of supreme confidence that comes from its unerring stability. In this respect, the Dunstall is, strangely, a most relaxing ride indeed.

The brilliant red head fairing is of an excellent design, and is an ideal compromise for the rider who doesn't want to encumber his machine with a full fairing. Also, a full fairing reflects engine noise upward and would take a merciless toll in day-in-day-out riding by way of rider fatigue. In event of an accident a full fairing may be damaged more easily, too. The

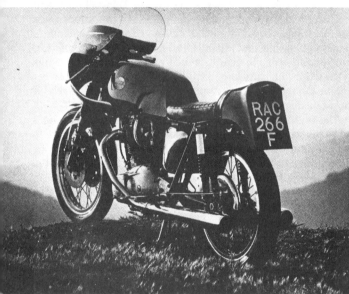

10-oz. grade fiberglass is not of the best quality and showed signs of vibration cracking, even away from mounting areas. It is thin, fabricated over the gel coat with a chopper gun, rather than being layed up on webbing. Web construction would be stronger, and resist vibration better when thin glass is used. Nonetheless, it is a valuable asset for high speed riding.

The braking abilities of the Dunstall Triumph must be experienced to be believed. While the rear brake is a stock Triumph unit, the front brake is a Lyster hydraulically operated twin-disc affair. The machine hauls down from 120 mph in a fantastically short distance. There is absolutely no fade, and therefore no fear of overshooting a fast turn, even when braking is delayed until the last millisecond. From lap to lap, the rider will not have to move his shut-off point backward from the turn to compensate for brake fade.

However, hydraulic operation, coupled with such brutal stopping power, poses a great danger for the uninitiated. Travel at the handle from "off" to wheel-locking tension is very short. There is no progressive feeling at all. This would make the brake extremely treacherous in the wet or similarly marginal traction conditions. There is no "feedback" from the braking surface through mechanical linkages to the lever, as there would be on a non-hydraulic brake. In other words, this brake is for the expert rider.

Cold starting the Dunstall was remarkably easy; just open

the fuel taps, tickle the concentrics, and one easy heave usually would light it. Unless the weather is cooler than 50-60 degrees the choke isn't needed. Warm starting takes more effort as it tends to flood more easily. About that choke. It is often necessary to wire these things open, as they are likely to vibrate to a partially shut position. A 15-minute ride will cause the lever to creep around sufficiently to inhibit performance and, naturally, gas mileage.

The Lucas electrical system worked flawlessly throughout the test. Spark is supplied to the NGK plugs by a Lucas capacitor ignition. Engine speeds reached 7500 rpm during the test without the slightest sign of incontinence from the unit. The horn, however, is something less than authoritative and it's highly unlikely that even the humblest of Detroit iron will cringe at its pusillanimous yelp. The ammeter is mounted in an instrument panel in the fairing, along with the speedometer and tachometer. The latter two dials are quite easy to read at speed and relatively immune to vibration of the fairing. Such is not the case with the ammeter, as its needle oscillates through almost every degree of its spectrum when the bike is underway. This, by the way, is not in the least unusual on machines equipped with ammeters. However, they are roughly indicative of charge or discharge rates when the bike is not moving.

A Dunstall Triumph carries relatively tall gearing, e.g. 103 mph in third. This is because Dunstall gears for the torque peak rather than peak horsepower. Besides yielding respectable gas mileage (40 mpg at 65 mph), high gearing allows high speed cruising at moderate engine revs. The bike's torque is very strong above 70 mph and will pull the machine up past "the ton" in a remarkably short time with nary a change in exhaust note. The gears are stock Bonneville touring ratios with the only changes being in final drive ratio and tire size. Riding easily, first gear starts require substantial clutch feathering. The gap between second and third gears is quite noticeable, although not bothersome. The machine would be clearly capable of 105-107 mph quarter-miles and low 12-sec. e.t.s were it geared for acceleration rather than road racing. The highest quarter-mile times were obtained using third gear through the trap, and the best e.t. was obtained by revving to peak torque and breaking the tire loose at the start. Shifting was done at 7200 rpm except for the second-to-third change which took place at 7400 rpm.

The increase from 649 to 744 cc is obtained by fitting the Dunstall aluminum barrel conversion to stock Triumph crankcases. The bore is enlarged from 71 to 76 mm while stroke remains unchanged at 82 mm. The cylinder head has been modified by way of enlarged, reshaped and polished ports. Bronze, Hi-Dural valve guides have been fitted along with special progressively wound valve springs, and the stock pistons have been exchanged for units which deliver a 10:1 compression ratio.

The cams are the stock grind used on the Bonneville and TR-6. The bike's somewhat cammy response is due to the headwork and raised compression. All in all, the engine's state of tune is far from inflexible, although lope is evident at idle. And while not in a perfect mechanical state, the Dunstall ran extremely strong when fully wound out to 7400 rpm. Because of this, the performance figures can be considered fairly representative.

With the fairing, alloy wheels, 4-gal. fiberglass fuel tank, clip-ons, and disc brake, a simple hot rod Triumph has assumed a mystic and fierce identity. It is surely less than an all-out racing bike but much more so than other street tourers. It appearance is so exalting, even the most apathetic personality would blink as it passes.

DUNSTALL 750 TRIUMPH

SPECIFICATIONS

List price	$1400 ex-works
Suspension, front	telescopic fork
Suspension, rear	swinging arm
Tire, front	3.00-19
Tire, rear	4.10-19
Brake, front, diameter x width, in.	9.125 x 1.562
Brake, rear, diameter x width, in.	7.0 x 1.13
Total brake swept area, sq. in.	65.0
Brake loading, lb./sq. in.	7.7
Engine, type	ohv vertical Twin
Bore x stroke, in., mm	2.937 x 3.230, 76 x 82
Piston displacement, cu. in., cc	45.4
Compression ratio	10.0:1
Carburetion	(2) 23-mm Amal concentric 930
Ignition	Lucas capacitor
Claimed bhp @ rpm	n.a.
Oil system	dry sump
Oil capacity, pt.	6.0
Fuel capacity, U.S. gal.	4.0
Recommended fuel	premium
Starting system	kick, folding crank
Lighting system	12-V alternator, diode rectifier
Air filtration	none
Clutch	multi-disc, wet
Primary drive	duplex chain
Final drive	single-row chain
Gear ratios, overall:1	
5th	none
4th	4.46
3rd	5.31
2nd	7.55
1st	10.9
Wheelbase, in.	56.75
Seat height, in.	31.0
Seat width, in.	10.5
Handlebar width, in.	21.0
Footpeg height, in.	11.0
Ground clearance, in.	5.75
Curb weight (w/half-tank fuel), lb.	363.0
Weight bias, front/rear, percent	53/47
Test weight (fuel and rider), lb.	518

TEST CONDITIONS

Air temperature, degrees F	72
Humidity, percent	66
Barometric pressure, in. Hg.	29.94
Altitude above mean sea level, ft.	350
Wind velocity, mph	4-8
Strip alignment, relative wind:	

```
            WIND
  S >------------------------> F
                      \
                       \
                        v
```

PERFORMANCE

Top speed (actual @ 7000 rpm), mph	123.21
Computed top speed in gears(@7000rpm),mph:	
5th	none
4th	123
3rd	100
2nd	70
1st	48
lph/1000 rpm, top gear	17
Engine revolutions/mile, top gear	3535
Piston speed (@7000rpm), ft./min.	3750
Fuel consumption, mpg	40.0
Speedometer error:	
50 mph indicated, actually	46.80
60 mph indicated, actually	56.25
70 mph indicated, actually	68.44
Braking distance:	
from 30 mph, ft.	26.2
from 60 mph, ft.	129.5
Acceleration, zero to:	
30 mph, sec.	2.7
40 mph, sec.	3.2
50 mph, sec.	4.2
60 mph, sec.	4.9
70 mph, sec.	5.7
80 mph, sec.	7.6
90 mph, sec.	9.3
100 mph, sec.	12.1
Standing one-eighth mile, sec.	7.69
terminal speed, mph	79.08
Standing one-quarter mile, sec.	13.44
terminal speed, mph	102.27

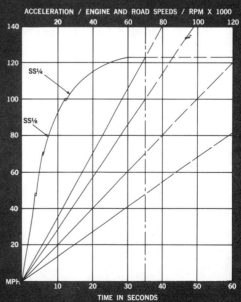

ACCELERATION / ENGINE AND ROAD SPEEDS / RPM X 1000

RICKMAN 8-VALVE TRIUMPH

It Turned the Quickest Quarter-Mile We've Ever Run And Has the Stopping Power of a Brick Wall.

THERE'S MAGIC in names. Success makes them magic. It begins when someone sticks his neck out—bare and clean on the chopping block—and culminates when the trials of time and experience set him free. Through hindsight such risks seem an easy price to pay, yet experience will always be the world's most valuable commodity.

Don and Derek Rickman earned their credentials this way—running the gauntlet of trials, motocrossing and road racing—and they've passed the benefits along to us; with, of course, their magic name.

The brothers had been considering the multiple-valve concept for the past few years. But it wasn't until late 1968 that a suitable design was finalized. Their main purpose was to produce a four-valve per cylinder conversion kit that would be equally at home on street or race track and yet remain within the commercial grasp of most motorcyclists.

The resulting product is a kit costing in the neighborhood of $550 that replaces almost all Triumph 650 engine components from the crankcase up, complete with special exhaust pipes and baffles. Indeed, the Triumph engine in standard trim is far from being a laggard, but this package brings out a sensationally savage soul.

To begin with, the Rickman cylinder barrel is a cast aluminum affair with pressed-in iron liners. The use of

aluminum here saves about 4 lb. over the standard iron cylinders, along with the obvious benefits of vastly improved cooling. It is also worth noting that because this weight is trimmed from a comparatively high portion of the machine, its center of gravity is lowered ever so slightly. It may not be much but every ounce gone contributes to more responsive handling.

Displacement has been enlarged to 683 cc, the result of a 2-mm increase in cylinder bore, and over-size pistons are supplied in the package. The standard pistons are conventional alloy castings which have proved entirely adequate for street use. But the Rickman approach forsakes these pieces for light alloy forged units which are better suited to the strains of competition.

And a good thing it is that these beefier pistons are included; the compression ratio has been raised from 9:1 to 11.5:1. At this stage thermal loadings, particularly under hard use, would likely prove too much for standard pistons. Needless to say, only the highest octane gasoline is prescribed; Standard Oil's Custom Supreme or Sunoco 260 should do well. A short fit of detonation could reduce these precision pieces to rubble—a dear price to pay for a moment's frugality at the gas station.

Before we move to other parts of the machine we should mention the leaky pushrod tubes. Oil seepage from this area is an old Triumph bugaboo. It occurs when the engine warms and various parts grow with heat. The thin wall steel tubing used for pushrod covers doesn't expand at the same rate of the cylinder and head at either end. Consequently, these parts grow away from each other, allowing untidy gaps for oil to ooze through. This problem could be eliminated by incorporating pushrod cavities in the cylinder casting. But as it stands, the standard Triumph pushrod tube is used in the Rickman kit

along with an adapter on the tube's upper end to compensate for the increased cylinder height. Later in the test, however, this gremlin was eliminated by the addition of four metal rings to supplement the standard neoprene O-rings. Each ring presses against a neoprene seal, exerting just a bit more pressure and taking up slack in the assembly.

Beneath the two finned rocker covers reside four polished rocker arms made of forged steel. Each rocker, while still activated by the standard Bonneville No. 3134 cams and pushrods, possesses two fingers to activate the valves, instead of one. Thus moving parts in the valve train are kept to a minimum. But while the number of valves in the head are doubled, the mass of each poppet is substantially less, lending to better control of inertial forces at high rpm.

Viewed from the standpoint of valve area, however, we discovered that the Rickman conversion actually provides *less* breathing area than the standard Triumph valves. The standard Triumph Bonneville intake and exhaust units measure 1-19/32 and 1-7/16 in. diameter respectively, and the Rickman valves are 1-1/8 and 1.0 in. diameter respectively. In terms of total breathing area, the standard parts yield 3.610 sq. in. while the Rickman parts offer 3.554 sq. in.

In light of this we can assume that the machine's sparkling performance is the product of several other factors: our test bike is more than 60 lb. lighter than a production Bonneville, a difference of almost 15 percent. Also, while the engine is far from being in full race tune, certain modifications add considerably to its output. These additions include increased compression and displacement along with larger carburetors. Such changes make a powerful combination in anyone's book.

The Rickman frame on our test bike is pretty much unchanged from the item last seen in the Street Metisse road test (CW July '68). This is not to say that chassis research and

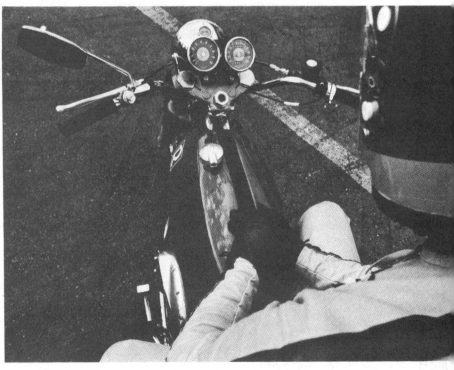

development has ground to a halt in Don and Derek's den, but that an excellent configuration has been attained, and for the time being, effort is now spent developing other components. Suffice it to say, the handsome nickle plated, bronze welded, Reynolds steel frame exemplifies the best precision of master craftsmen. It is rigid, and handling is extremely stable, over anything from pockmarks to railroad tracks.

In keeping with the machine's tenor, a giant 10-in. diameter Lockheed disc brake is fitted to the Rickman front fork. This unit is extremely smooth and responsive, demanding neither uncomfortably high pressure at the lever nor the sensitive touch of a GP veteran to achieve optimum braking efficiency. Nor did repeated high speed applications result in sponginess or chatter as pucks and disc absorb the energy of the hurtling machine.

A disc binder is also implemented at the rear wheel. But because it is operated by one's foot, and because said foot is not so sensitive as the hand, more care is warranted when using it. To avoid locking the rear wheel light application is advised.

It would be a great injustice to omit praise of the bike's superlative brakes. During the test they achieved the shortest 60 mph-to-0 stopping distance ever recorded by this magazine. Now, if this machine were a super-pizazz road racer weighing a hundred pounds less or so, our astonishment might be mitigated. But the Rickman Triumph, replete with fiberglass accoutrements, is a street bike tipping the scales at 359 lb.!

Adding to its credentials as a State-Of-The-Art motorcycle are the quarter-mile acceleration figures. The Rickman Triumph thundered through the clocks with a 13.08-sec. elapsed time and 102.50 mph. Ensuring that this was no fluke recording, the bike again zapped down the strip. This time it registered 104.16 mph in 13.11 sec.! By a comfortable margin this is the quickest and fastest accelerating motorcycle tested by CYCLE WORLD.

Which brings us to another point. Contemporary thought has always placed the value of such multi-valve arrangements in the upper rpm ranges where valve control is so critical. But as the test machine was redlined at 7000 rpm and utilized box stock cams, that dictum has been effectively blown into the weeds. Obviously, the engine's breathing is vastly improved along the entire rpm scale rather than merely after the point of conventional value failure.

Starting the Rickman Triumph is a good deal easier than anticipated. The specter of that 11.5:1 compression ratio and a pair of 32-mm Amal Concentric carburetors (stock units are 30 mm) does little to encourage first kick starts. But the machine lights with surprisingly little effort. Seldom is more than two dabs at the starter lever necessary to bring the bike to life.

Incidentally, these larger carburetors are included in the Rickman eight-valve kit as are all the vital gaskets, nuts, bolts and studs. Offered optionally are two 34-mm carburetors and manifold along with a special exhaust system, boosting output an additional 5 bhp to 70 bhp at 7000 rpm. For this latter stage of tune the Rickmans recommend that the crankshaft be endowed with more stamina through heat treating and that a special gear type oil pump be added. Otherwise, in the interest of long term reliability, the brothers advise a 7000-rpm rev limit. In the upper end, however, Derek Rickman indicated that the valve gear is capable of 9000 rpm with safety.

Inveterate dreamers that we are, images of a robust Rickman lower end conversion fill our heads like sugar plums. Just imagine, an eight-valve large displacement Twin with 9000 rpm reliability—a short step away from a street-GP hike! ◙

RICKMAN 8-VALVE TRIUMPH

SPECIFICATIONS

List price . . . . $550 (for kit only)
Suspension, front . . . . telescopic fork
Suspension, rear . . . . swinging arm
Tire, front . . . . Dunlop K81, 4.10-18
Tire, rear . . . . Dunlop K81, 4.10-18
Brake, front, diameter x width, in. . . 10.0 x 3.0
Brake, rear, diameter x width, in. . . . 10.0 x 3.0
Total brake swept area, sq. in. 188.4
Brake loading, lb./sq. in. 2.78
Engine, type . . . . ohv vertical Twin
Bore x stroke, in., mm . . . . 2.87 x 3.23, 73 x 82
Piston displacement, cu. in., cc 41.6, 683
Compression ratio 11.5:1
Carburetion . . . . . . (2) 32-mm Amal Concentric
Ignition . . . . 12-V battery and coil
Claimed bhp @ rpm . . . . 64.8 @ 7000
Oil system . . . . dry sump
Oil capacity, pt. 7.0
Fuel capacity, U.S. gal. 4.2
Recommended fuel . . . . premium
Starting system . . . . kick, folding crank
Lighting system 12V
Air filtration . . . . none
Clutch . . . . multi-disc, wet
Primary drive . . . . duplex chain
Final drive . . . . 5/8-in. x 3/8-in. chain
Gear ratios, overall: 1
   5th . . . . none
   4th 4.80
   3rd 5.71
   2nd 8.10
   1st 11.70
Wheelbase, in. 56.1
Seat height, in. 30.6
Seat width, in. 8.3
Handlebar width, in. 32.0
Footpeg height, in. 11.5
Ground clearance, in. 5.8
Curb weight (w/half-tank fuel), lb. 359
Weight bias, front/rear, percent 50/50
Test weight (fuel and rider), lb. 523

TEST CONDITIONS

Air temperature, degrees F 88
Humidity, percent 35
Barometric pressure, in. Hg. 30.01
Altitude above mean sea level, ft. 350
Wind velocity, mph 3-5
Strip alignment, relative wind:

WIND
S ▶————————————————▶ F

PERFORMANCE

Top speed (actual @ 7240 rpm), mph . . . 111.26
Computed top speed in gears (@ 7200 rpm), mph:
   5th . . . . none
   4th 110
   3rd 93
   2nd 66
   1st 38
Mph/1000 rpm, top gear 15.35
Engine revolutions/mile, top gear 3910
Piston speed (@ 7200 rpm), ft./min. 3880
Fuel consumption, mpg 31
Speedometer error:
   50 mph indicated, actually 45.63
   60 mph indicated, actually 55.04
   70 mph indicated, actually 64.42
Braking distance:
   from 30 mph, ft. 27
   from 60 mph, ft. 99
Acceleration, zero to:
   30 mph, sec. 2.4
   40 mph, sec. 3.7
   50 mph, sec. 4.1
   60 mph, sec. 5.0
   70 mph, sec. 6.8
   80 mph, sec. 7.9
   90 mph, sec. 9.1
   100 mph, sec. 11.9
Standing one-eighth mile, sec. 8.37
   terminal speed, mph 84.04
Standing one-quarter mile, sec. 13.11
   terminal speed, mph 104.16

ACCELERATION / ENGINE AND ROAD SPEEDS / RPM X 100

SS¼

SS⅛

TIME IN SECONDS

TRIUMPH TROPHY 500

Triumph's Finest, After 32 Years, Is Still Triumph's Finest, But How Much Longer Can It Endure?

WHO NEEDS A 500 Triumph? After all, horsepower is where it's at, right? You pay a little more for a 650 or 750 and you get your bhp. It's that simple.

Sorry, but we don't agree. We have a certain feeling about the 500. Partly because 500 cc is the classic limit in international competition, and was the mainstay of AMA "Class C" racing until 1969. It's an economical size, big enough to thrill, yet compact enough to be an extension of man's spirit.

That feeling runs even deeper. Down to archetypal level. If the dentist gave us sodium pentothal we wouldn't babble about 650s or 750s. Our hazy reveries would be all 500s. And particularly the 500 Triumph.

Ivan remembers... He raced a kitted Tiger at the Island in 1952. Before that he had a sprung hub 1948 Tiger 100, which he cafe-raced on the roads of back country Canada.

"For its day, it was smooth, handled reasonably well and had good brakes. (Crafty smile.) There was nobody on the road from Belleville to Kingston who could stay with me. (Frown.) No, I better not say that—we've got a safety image to keep up."

"Aw come on, Ivan, it's only a reverie."

"Okay, okay. (Smile.) Make that: nobody stayed with me, day *or night*. Hah!"

Clutch remembers. "It was my everything bike. I raced it in Class C, 500 Sportsman, and cow-trailed on it. I liked a lighter bike. I once traded a 40 straight across for a T100C. It's part of the club of growing up. You have to have a 500 Triumph. Funny, what turned me on about it. The way it spins the rear wheel. Doesn't accomplish a damn thing, but it makes your heart go 'woooo!' "

Dan remembers his 10 months straight on a '62 in the wilds of Europe. The image still lingers—the shocked faces of two carabinieri, fumbling to start their Guzzis, as a joyous levi-clad American wearing an odd red jersey flashed by on a dirt road detour, showering gravel. "Oh, the way you could pitch that thing on those windy European roads!"

And then there's Joe. Matchless Joe. Maico Joe. Ducati Joe Metisse. A lover of Singles. But he admits that he, too, had a Trophy, back in '49.

"I loved it. Lots of power, and it shifted good. And I liked the sound. I had it all chromed and decked out in red ignition wire—you remember, like all the guys used to do. Then I'd go out in the dirt and beat hell out of it. I remember riding an enduro at Calabasas and almost getting castrated on the luggage rack. (Wistful pause.) Yes indeedy, it was a girl pleaser."

Joe doesn't have to worry about the luggage rack. It's gone. A "refinement" in reverse. But that 500 Twin is still here, a design conceived 32 years ago. Enough years and memories to make it a relic. Overshadowed as it is by its bigger brethren, the 500 has somehow persisted. Perhaps it owes its continued existence to American racing, culminating with Triumph's big assault on Daytona in 1966 and 1967. Except for the massive effort to improve the Daytona racer's handling and performance—things which were passed along to the production models—the 500 would be just another 500. Today, it is still

Triumph's finest machine. A basically sound and well proportioned design.

There are two 500 Triumphs. The T100R Daytona roadster with dual carburetors and low mufflers is the fastest, capable of 90-mph quarters in the 14s and 105-mph top speed. Yet the single carburetor, high pipe T100C "Trophy" is more popular in spite of lesser performance. Versatility is what sells it. The Trophy 500 handles as well or better than any production road bike made. Stripped of lights, and regeared, it makes an excellent cow-trailer or fireroad machine, good enough to win the national enduro championship for seven straight years.

An initiate to the 1970 version of the T100C will likely be impressed, first of all, with the bike's quiet smoothness. It purrs docilely around town below 50 mph, and pulls easily at low rpm. This latter characteristic makes the bike easy for the novice to ride (and a welcome relief to those who are used to keeping the revs up to get torque). Mechanical noise is fairly low. Surprising, as the cylinder barrel appears to be aluminum, like the head and cases. But it is really iron, which absorbs noise.

Over 55 mph, the purr becomes a buzz. This, of course, is the reason for the popularity of the bigger 650, which only has to turn 3500 rpm at 65 mph and therefore gives a more relaxed sensation than the 500 at that speed. However, the buzz of a 500 is nowhere near as disconcerting as that of a 650 running at the same engine speed. The 500 is a better balanced engine, with lighter pistons, rods and valve gear. The displacement is near ideal for a Twin. "Oversquare" bore/stroke dimensions (69 by 65.5 mm), instituted in 1959 along with in-unit transmission, also make it an inherently smoother and more efficient machine than the long-stroke (71 by 82 mm) 650 Twin. After you get over the initial apprehensions having to do with turning an engine at high rpm, you'll find that the T100C buzz remains pretty much the same at 85 mph as it is at 55 mph. Sweet music. And the bike won't complain about being run all day at 70 mph.

The engine has a hidden dual nature. You could ride all day and never know about it. Then, one day, you decide to "let her wind." And bang, a whole new rush of power comes in at about 5000 rpm and lasts to about 7500 rpm when the valves begin to float. Fantastic. Good low rpm torque, yet an almost cammy rush at 5000 rpm. This is a characteristic of Triumph's Q-profile camshaft, which was incorporated in the 500 in 1963. It is now used in both the 30- and 40-inchers, but that "Q" effect seems most pronounced in the 500s, which have a "hemi" type head designed by Doug Hele for the Daytona racers and subsequently adopted in the T100R in 1967. It wasn't until 1969 that the T100C got the benefit of the new head.

Now it takes the mere addition of a bolt-on manifold and a second carburetor to bring the T100C head up to T100R specifications. But there is still one important difference. The hotter T100R uses the Q-cam for both intake and exhaust, where the T100C uses the Q-cam for the intake only, and a milder N-type cam for the exhaust.

Bearing similarity to the Jomo "scrambles" cam (or, in the East, the TriCor "Daytona" cam) used by Gary Nixon in his 500-cc flattrackers, the Q-type cam can be described as moderately sporty, with 269 degrees duration. Intake opens 34 btc, closes 55 abc. Lift is .314 in. By comparison, the flattracker cam has only 8 degrees more duration and .313-in. lift. The N-type profile is used in the T100C exhaust cam mainly to shorten intake/exhaust overlap, i.e., the time both intake and exhaust valves are open simultaneously. Shorter overlap makes the engine more useful at lower rpm for off-road riding.

Duration of the N-type cam is shorter, at 255 degrees, with exhaust opening at 48 degrees bbc and closing 27 degrees atc. Lift is also milder at .296 in. Comparing overlap of the two T100s is useful: in the R, where two Q-type cams are used, overlap is 68 degrees; in the C model, utilizing Q intake and N exhaust, it is 51 degrees.

Triumph cam faces in the past have not been noted for extreme longevity, but the situation has greatly improved since the manufacturers adopted a nitriding process to harden the cam lobes in 1969.

Some T100s may exhibit a slight fluffiness or lag just before the upper power band is reached, as did our test machine. This has nothing to do with the cam design, but is caused by the Amal Concentric carburetor running slightly rich. Reducing main jet size slightly or dropping the needle a position will eliminate the lag effect.

While the T100s have not undergone any major design changes since the appearance of the unit transmission, they are regularly improved, the changes rarely being announced. Most recently, to reduce wear, the timing side of the crankshaft has been converted to run on ball bearings, as do the 650s, rather than plain bearings. The drive side now runs on roller bearings. Lubrication is now similar to the 650s: oil is pumped to the crankshaft timing side by use of a disc in the timing cover, and exits through two holes in each journal to lubricate the big ends, which ride on plain bearing inserts. There is no bushing on the small end of the rod.

The crankcase breathing system used on the Daytona racers is now standard production practice in the T100C. Rather than employing the usual timed breather, the crankcase vents to the primary chaincase. This is accomplished by eliminating the oil seal on the drive side main bearing, allowing air pressure and oil mist to vent through the bearings to the chaincase. Three 1/16-inch holes in the crankshaft chamber wall allow excess oil to dribble back from the chaincase to the sump.

An important benefit of this system is that the primary chaincase can never run dry; proper oil level is automatically maintained. This is rather clever engineering when you think about it. Eliminate the expense of two parts, oil seal and breather, and gain a simple form of automatic oiling at the same time.

Another area of minor improvement is in the transmission, which has always been one of the T100's strongest points in terms of lightness and smoothness. Gas carburizing is used to harden transmission gears, resulting not only in longer life, but quieter running. Why the gears should run quieter is not immediately apparent, but the hardening process does result in a smoother finish on mating surfaces, which would make for quieter meshing.

As for chassis and suspension, they benefit from several improvements in recent years. In 1967, the diameter of the front down tube was increased for greater strength and the fork rake increased 1 degree, both useful for dirt application. At this time, the swinging arm was beefed up after experimentation with the Daytona racers. These improvements are greatly responsible for the 500's stability on the road and its precise steering. The springing at the rear is just about perfect for road riding, but acts somewhat spongy if you hang slides on your favorite fireroad. Chances are that stripping the bike for the dirt, which will bring the machine down to about 330 lb., would have the effect of making springing more properly stiff.

The front forks are excellent, damp well, and contribute much to the bike's good handling. On the 1970 model, the practice of finishing-grinding and chroming the stanchions has been added, to improve the function of the oil seals. Dirt riders will welcome the wider handlebars, the same as those on the 650s, replacing the narrow bars of yore which were usually the first item a T100 owner would unload.

While we're at it, here are a few other 1970 detail improvements: carburetor mounted on a rubber O-ring to prevent fuel frothing; a better air filter, four-ply instead of two; adjustable sidestand folding to allow hard leaning types to get it up out of the way; easier access to rear damper adjustment holes; mirror bracket mounting integral with hand lever assemblies.

While never-ending refinement such as this has made the T100 Triumph's finest achievement, you wonder whether they haven't forgotten something. The problem is rather akin to the evolution of the old Leica. It started out light and compact. You could put it in your pocket. That was its virtue. But it got heavier, and bigger. Nowadays, nobody sticks a Leica M4 in his pocket.

Likewise, The T100C has gained about 20 lb. in the last few years. Before that, it was even lighter. Some of the weight comes from the second muffler; add a few ounces for the flimsy trellis which guards milady's leg. Frankly, we would rather burn milady's leg, but fortunately for her, we are not in the majority. The second muffler, of course, provides the required degree of silent legality, while retaining exhaust efficiency. But it would be nice to see development of a single, lighter silencer that could do the same thing.

Aiming closer to the 300-lb. mark would serve to better differentiate the 500 from the 650. This, plus the addition of a five-speed gearbox, would serve to increase the appeal of both C and R models beyond the devoted coterie of road riding purists and four-stroke trail buffs who now comprise the bulk of its market.

As it is, the T100C is poetry. Superb road handling. A modicum of convertibility for the dirt. Excellent braking, requiring only one or two fingers on the front stopper. Easy starting. And exemplary reliability. But in terms of development, the T100 is at the same stage as the Austin-Healey sports car (although it's a darn sight better than the Healey will ever be). Both have been refined so conservatively, that they are on the verge of extinction.

Simply, we'd like to see the 500 evolve. And thereby endure. We can see its virtues, tangible and intangible. But can the mass market see? They are not so devoted as we are.

TRIUMPH TROPHY 500

SPECIFICATIONS

List price	$1160 p.o.e. West Coast
Suspension, front	telescopic fork
Suspension, rear	swinging arm
Tire, front	3.25-19
Tire, rear	4.00-18
Brake, front, diameter x width, in.	7.0 x 1.1
Brake, rear, diameter x width, in.	7.0 x 1.1
Total brake swept area, sq. in.	49.7
Brake loading, lb./sq. in.	10.7
Engine, type	ohv vertical Twin
Bore x stroke, in., mm	2.72 x 2.58, 69 x 65
Piston displacement, cu. in., cc	30, 490
Compression ratio	9.0:1
Carburetion	(1) Amal Concentric 26 mm
Ignition	battery and coil
Claimed bhp @ rpm	38 @ 7000
Oil system	dry sump
Oil capacity, pt.	6.0
Fuel capacity, U.S. gal.	2.25
Recommended fuel	premium
Starting system	kick, folding crank
Lighting system	12-V alternator
Air filtration	washable, pleated cloth
Clutch	multi-disc, wet
Primary drive	duplex chain
Final drive	5/8-in. x 3/8-in. chain
Gear ratios, overall:1	
5th	none
4th	5.70
3rd	6.90
2nd	9.20
1st	14.10
Wheelbase, in.	54.5
Seat height, in.	32.0
Seat width, in.	10.5
Handlebar width, in.	32.0
Footpeg height, in.	11.0
Ground clearance, in.	7.5
Curb weight (w/half-tank fuel), lb.	369
Weight bias, front/rear, percent	44/56
Test weight (fuel and rider), lb.	534

TEST CONDITIONS

Air temperature, degrees F	75
Humidity, percent	60
Barometric pressure, in. Hg.	30.01
Altitude above mean sea level, ft.	350
Wind velocity, mph	5-7
Strip alignment, relative wind:	

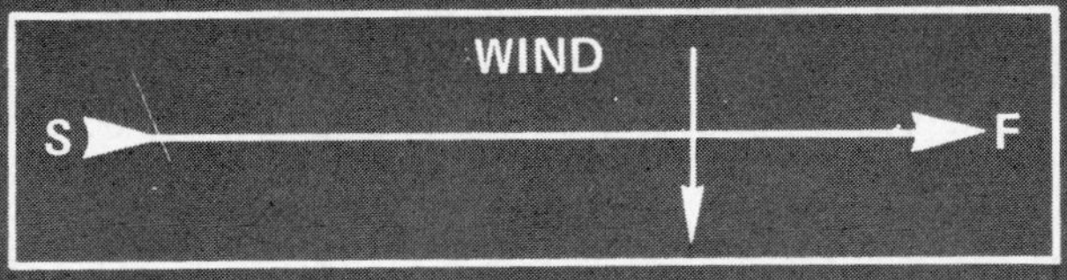

WIND

S ———> F

PERFORMANCE

Top speed (actual @ 6876 rpm), mph	93.87
Computed top speed in gears(@7800rpm), mph:	
5th	none
4th	101
3rd	88
2nd	66
1st	43
Mph/1000 rpm, top gear	13.65
Engine revolutions/mile, top gear	4400
Piston speed (@ 7800 rpm), ft./min.	3350
Fuel consumption, mpg	44
Speedometer error:	
50 mph indicated, actually	51.54
60 mph indicated, actually	62.11
70 mph indicated, actually	72.28
Braking distance:	
from 30 mph, ft.	33
from 60 mph, ft.	124
Acceleration, zero to:	
30 mph, sec.	2.8
40 mph, sec.	4.0
50 mph, sec.	5.9
60 mph, sec.	7.6
70 mph, sec.	10.0
80 mph, sec.	13.5
90 mph, sec.	20.8
100 mph, sec.	
Standing one-eighth mile, sec.	10.25
terminal speed, mph	70.58
Standing one-quarter mile, sec.	15.50
terminal speed, mph	84.98

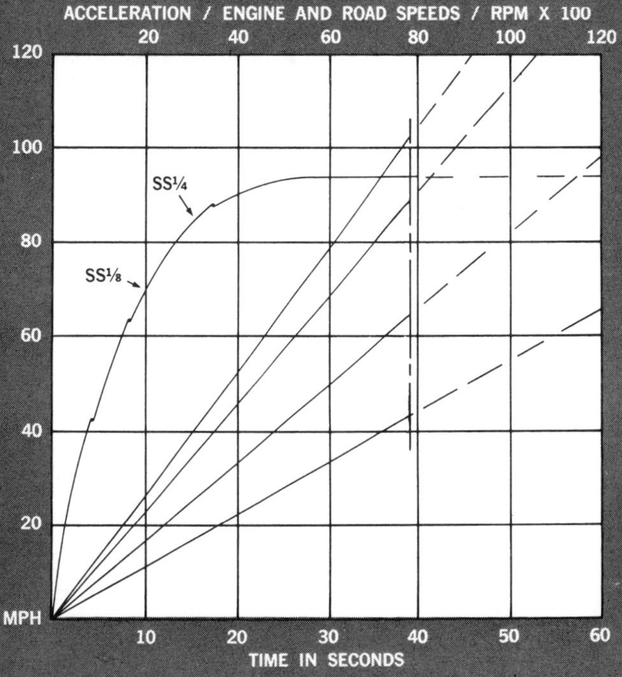

ACCELERATION / ENGINE AND ROAD SPEEDS / RPM X 100

SS¼

SS⅛

TIME IN SECONDS

TRIUMPH 250 TROPHY

Slow, But Friendly

IF TRIUMPH THOUGHT they were going to get a corner on the performance market with their diminutive 250-cc Trophy, it would not be unfair to accuse them of missing the boat. Perform, it does not.

However, the Trophy does have a definite place in motorcycling. It is not a failure, but rather a victim of a somewhat lopsided, or even demented, American market. The majority of buyers of street machinery are active, hyper-thyroid types who want the most go-power they can get for their dollar. But there exists a gap that most 250s sold in the U.S. do not fill. The Trophy 250 does.

Did you ever wish for a machine mild-mannered enough that you could completely ignore it as you plonked about town? One that didn't require constant attention from the throttle hand in the interest of maintaining the legal speed in a business or residential area? One that had enough flywheel effect at slow speed in the higher gears to prevent the constant jerking forward and back of the rider? One that would still be passable for short trips at freeway speeds, even though you'd have to forego longer voyages (unless you were a mechanical wizard)? And finally, a machine that you could leave the road with to indulge in some mild cow trailing?

The Trophy 250 does all these things. And it does them calmly, because it is a 250 four-stroke Single, of ancient heritage.

It is for the guy who has peace of mind, and wants to keep it. It is for the guy who has "made it." He needs to prove

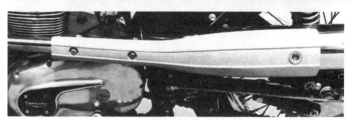

nothing. He merely wants a motorcycle for "messing around," or for getting him down to the beach when he doesn't want to take his Shelby GT or his Lamborghini.

Remarkably simple in design and constructed like an armored car, the Trophy 250 should require only minimal service and adjustments, making it an ideal machine for the occasional rider.

Despite its heavy weight, the Trophy is very maneuverable and stable, even when packing double. Many of the components are taken directly from the larger BSA and Triumph models, which help increase the weight as well as the strength. Front forks look exactly like the units found on the Trophy 500 and feel as though the springs are the same: stiff! Rear suspension is stiff, too, but handling is much the better for it. Despite a trace of front end wag at high speeds, the Trophy 250 could be heeled into corners at a good clip and still impart a sense of security. The Dunlop K-70 tires must take some of the credit, as they were almost impossible to break loose while cornering on the pavement. They also make fairly good off-the-road tires for occasional trailing.

The engine is an overhead valve design which was originally conceived as the 150-cc Terrier in 1954. It then grew to 200cc and was called the Tiger Cub. BSA then picked up the ball and slightly redesigned the Cub and came up with the C-15 Star in 1958, and a scrambles version followed the next year. A trials model soon appeared, and the lightweight gained in popularity like the VW.

BSA continued production of the C-15 and enlarged it to 350cc and finally to the present 441cc of the Victor. Meanwhile, Triumph had only the little 200 Tiger Cub which, with the exception of the 250-cc Twin Tigress scooter, was their only lightweight.

BSA felt that it was time to revamp the C-15 and did so with the result being named the B-25. Triumph dropped the Tiger Cub from production and, as a result of a tighter merger with BSA, unveiled the TR25W, which is practically a carbon-copy of the B-25, with the exception of styling features. Many of the good features of both marques are evident in this lightweight, and some of the not-so-good ones too.

We especially liked the neat appearance of the rear shock absorbers and the quickly-detachable rear wheel assembly which makes it unnecessary to break the rear chain when changing the rear tire. Paint is beautifully applied and what chrome there is, is of excellent quality. Polished aluminum abounds on the engine, and even the fin edges have received the buffing wheel. Engine castings are quite smooth and evidently better machined than earlier models. Ours hardly leaked any oil at all.

The latest version has a forged one-piece crankshaft and a two-piece connecting rod with replaceable babbit inserts as in the larger Triumphs. In fact, the bore/stroke ratio is the same as on the Trident 750.

A double-gear oil pump circulates engine oil from the tank

through the engine and passes through two rather coarse strainers, one in the bottom of the tank and the other in the sump by the pump. Oil for the overhead valve rocker mechanism is taken from a bleed tube in the return oil line. Both the transmission and the primary chaincase have their own oil supplies, with the primary's being used to lubricate the rear chain.

The engine is somewhat noisy, with considerable valve clatter as in earlier models. This is due to the fact that there are no ribs cast between the fins to help deaden the racket. But, ribs would be less attractive than no ribs, and one gets accustomed to the din rather quickly. It made all of us nostalgic, but we know of one tester who would put plastic buttons between his fins!

A rather sporty camshaft lifts the valves using relatively short pushrod assemblies which terminate into rocker arms with no adjusting screws. The rocker arm spindles are eccentric, and adjustment is accomplished by rotating them slightly until the correct valve clearance is obtained, without the need for the slightly heavier screw and nut arrangement found on most four cycles. The little engine revs quite happily over the 8000-rpm mark without valve float, but it must be kept revving to get much power out of it. It is happy enough when pottering about town in the higher gears, but power is lacking.

Four-speed gearboxes are practically passe these days where five-and six-speeders abound, but the Trophy's gear ratios are

so well placed that more gears really aren't necessary. Shifting was quick and positive, neutral easy to find. Clutch action is light, thanks to the worm-gear disengaging mechanism, and shocks from the power impulses of the engine are effectively damped by rubber discs in the clutch hub. The clutch stood up well under the fairly heavy slipping it was subjected to while we were trying out the off-roadability. This was where the stiff suspension really paid off. It was practically impossible to bottom the forks and the wheels were able to follow the ground irregularities quite well. We did feel that a steering damper would be beneficial for this type of going, however.

Controls are well laid out, in British fashion, with the shift on the right and rear brake on the left. Handlebars are just right for the type of riding most Americans do, but were a trifle high for high-speed riding. The throttle is a quick-acting unit which requires only a quarter-turn to open fully. Headlight dimmer switch and horn button are located on the left handlebar, conveniently close to the rider's thumb. The headlight switch nestles between the high-beam indicator and the oil pressure warning lights in the center of the headlight.

Starting was a simple matter, even on cool mornings. Simply turn on the gas valve, tickle the carburetor until the float bowl overflows, and give the kickstarter a deliberate prod. It rarely took more than two kicks to get it going and only a minute or so before it would run smoothly. Lighting was excellent, and all the electrics performed splendidly. Even the horn was audible.

Plonking around town was a delight. With more than adequate brakes and easy-to-operate controls, threading one's way through 5 o'clock traffic was child's play. Once on the freeway, however, it was necessary to keep the engine buzzing to get with the traffic. Muffling is quite good with a silencer as large as on the 650 Triumph twins, but the heat guard was very uncomfortable for the passenger and looked rather out of place. It is made of fiberglass(!) and is a metalflake silver color which didn't really go with any other color on the machine.

A nice feature was the oil pressure warning light on the headlight, the sending unit for which was located on the right-hand side near the front of the crankcase. As soon as the check ball lifts off its seat, the light extinguishes, but with all the chrome on the headlight, it was difficult to tell whether it was burning or not because of the sun's reflection.

The blending of so many big motor components is done rather skillfully, but we were stumped as to why the front spokes should be one-third again as large as the rear spokes and why the springing should be so stiff. There was no provision for a center stand, either.

We all enjoyed riding the Trophy 250 and would like to see more four-stroke Singles in production. There's something about riding one that you can't forget.

TRIUMPH 250 TROPHY

SPECIFICATIONS

List price	$755 West Coast
Suspension, front	telescopic fork
Suspension, rear	swinging arm
Tire, front	3.25-18
Tire, rear	4.00-18
Brake, front, diameter x width, in.	7.0 x 1.125
Brake, rear, diameter x width, in.	7.0 x 1.125
Total brake swept area, sq. in.	49.5
Brake loading, lb./sq. in.	10.26
Engine, type	ohv Single
Bore x stroke, in., mm	2.67 x 2.75, 67 x 70
Piston displacement, cu. in., cc	15, 249
Compression ratio	10:1
Carburetion	Amal concentric 28-mm
Ignition	battery and coil
Claimed bhp @ rpm	22 @ 8200
Oil system	gear pump, dry sump
Oil capacity, pt.	4.8
Fuel capacity, U.S. gal.	3.9
Recommended fuel	premium
Starting system	kick, folding crank
Lighting system	battery, alternator
Air filtration	washable gauze
Clutch	multi-disc, wet
Primary drive	duplex chain
Final drive	single-row chain
Gear ratios, overall:1	
5th	none
4th	7.38
3rd	9.18
2nd	12.16
1st	19.59
Wheelbase, in.	53
Seat height, in.	32
Seat width, in.	11
Handlebar width, in.	27
Footpeg height, in.	13
Ground clearance, in.	8.5
Curb weight (w/half-tank fuel), lb.	348
Weight bias, front/rear, percent	43/57
Test weight (fuel and rider), lb.	508

TEST CONDITIONS

Air temperature, degrees F	70
Humidity, percent	77
Barometric pressure, in. Hg.	29.95
Altitude above mean sea level, ft.	50
Wind velocity, mph	10-15
Strip alignment, relative wind:	

```
                  WIND
 S  ►───────────────────────────►  F
```

PERFORMANCE

Top speed (actual @ 7900 rpm), mph	82.72
Computed top speed in gears (@ 8200 rpm),mph:	
5th	none
4th	86
3rd	69
2nd	52
1st	31
Mph/1000 rpm, top gear	10.5
Engine revolutions/mile, top gear	5701
Piston speed (@ 8200 rpm), ft./min.	3752
Speedometer error:	
50 mph indicated, actually	46.99
60 mph indicated, actually	56.96
70 mph indicated, actually	66.27
Braking distance:	
from 30 mph, ft.	25.4
from 60 mph, ft.	114.9
Acceleration, zero to:	
30 mph, sec.	2.8
40 mph, sec.	4.3
50 mph, sec.	6.0
60 mph, sec.	9.6
70 mph, sec.	14.9
80 mph, sec.	26.5
Standing one-eighth mile, sec.	10.2
terminal speed, mph	61.8
Standing one-quarter mile, sec.	17.7
terminal speed, mph	73.3

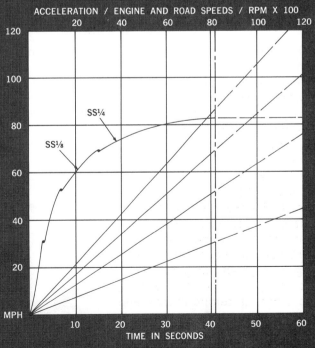

ACCELERATION / ENGINE AND ROAD SPEEDS / RPM X 100

A breed apart.

The Trident 750

The best Triumph yet. The culmination of 68 years of unrivalled experience and achievement. Not a copy, not a refinement, but an original ...designed from the stand up. A machine bred to win. Created for the man who loves to ride.

Three transverse vertical cylinders for a silky-smooth, vibration-free ride that has to be felt to be believed. 750cc's of power that put you out front and keep you there. Three 27mm Amal concentric carburetors for ultra precision fuel feed. Specially designed, high efficiency oil radiator (aircraft type) to maintain lower engine running temperatures and lengthen engine life. Four speed super smooth transmission (automotive type single plate clutch). New eight-inch

air-scooped, twin leading shoe front brake and seven-inch rear brake for that extra margin of safety. Completely new Dunlop Trigonic rear tire with buttressed tread pattern to meet the Trident's high performance re-

quirements. Unique top mounted, vibration-free instrument binnacle. And a number of other design innovations that make this Triumph the standard by which all the others are judged.

But features are one thing and performance another. And here's where the Trident really shines. For performance is bred into every Triumph. The kind of performance that sets records and then goes ahead to break them. The kind of performance that enabled the Triumph Trident 750 to take an unprecedented 15 out of 16 events in its class at Bonneville last year.

If you have to be ahead of the rest get way ahead on the Trident 750.

Triumph East, P.O. Box 6790, Baltimore, Md. 2120
Triumph West, P.O. Box 275, Duarte, Calif. 91010

The New BSA/TRIUMPH 350

Technical Analysis Of An All-New Twin From Great Britain. Features: Double Overhead Cam, Five-Speed Gearbox And Frame Styled After The Daytona Racing 750s.

TEXT AND PHOTOS BY DAN HUNT

THOSE WHO HAVE decried England's conservative approach to motorcycle design will undoubtedly carp that the new five-speed dohc 350 gracing the 1971 BSA and Triumph lines is five years too late. But the 350 is remarkable nonetheless, and, discounting the usual number of British design eccentricities, thoroughly up to date.

It is exciting, in fact. The old BSA and Triumph pushrod Twins have been around a long time. They are good machines and demand nodding respect in that they have endured, with minimal updating and refinement, for about three decades. The new 350 is the incarnation of what we supposed the next step would be—a step long delayed by Great Britain's low-key, post-war economic climate.

The new 350 Twin is not a copy of the Japanese Honda 350. Rather, it is a logical extension of what came before. Even in terms of styling, the BSA/Triumph combine has avoided looking over its shoulder to the Orient and instead carried the functional look characteristic of the big Twins and factory racing Threes into this sporty, businesslike double knocker. For styling and mechanical appeal, if nothing else, the new 350 does for BSA and Triumph what the XKE did for Jaguar.

The engine, an eye-catching component on this new machine, recalls the rich tradition of racing Manxes, G50s and 7Rs, with the double overhead cam boxes and massive tower for the cam driver. Its cylinders are canted forward about 15 degrees, allowing it to be stuffed into a compact, low-slung frame, and yet leaving room for the extra engine height created by the two cam boxes.

Why the designers chose to adopt the relatively complex double overhead camshaft design over the lighter and less bulky single overhead cam, or even the pushrod system, is a matter of speculation. A high-rpm dohc engine has the obvious advantages of minimized valve train "slop" and better cylinder head cooling because of the open area between the cam boxes. As fuel charge flow is best served by inclined valves, which reduce the bending of intake and exhaust ports into the combustion chamber, the separate disposition of overhead cams facilitates such valve inclination. If you want to incline the valves to any great degree in a sohc or pushrod engine, you are faced with providing rather lanky connective rigamarole—rockers, etc.—necessary to open the valve from a remotely located cam. As the cams work directly on inverted bucket-type cam followers in the 350's dohc design, there is bound to be less play and therefore greater accuracy in valve timing, as well as less valve train inertia.

So we have straight porting, inclined valves, minimal valve train "slop" and low inertia. Is all this really necessary on a production machine that produces 34 bhp at 9000 rpm from 349cc, or, in terms of specific output, 98 bhp per liter? There are times that Triumph and BSA have argued that it isn't, the most recent being when they expounded on their reasons for using pushrods in the 750-cc, three-cylinder engine. As a sidelight, you'll recall Honda's turnabout when they created the dohc 450 Twin and then retreated to a sohc layout in the

later 325-cc Twin, which revs quite nicely to 11,000 rpm, connective rigamarole and all.

The point of this discussion is that, in valve train design, there are no hard and fast rules. "Good" is what works and can be manufactured and sold profitably. Probably, the most logical explanation of BSA/Triumph's choice is that the designers wanted to come up with the horniest engine design possible, and double overhead cams were the horniest thing they could think of.

Drive to the camshafts is accomplished by one single-row chain, rather than gears or toothed belts, to keep engine width to a minimum. The chain, traveling in an inverted "L" pattern, is tensioned on its upward vertical run by a Weller blade, a curved clip of spring steel which may be adjusted for slack by loosening one bolt and moving the tensioner rearward on its mounting slots. This operation is somewhat more complex than the outside adjustment on the comparable Honda Twin, as the Triumph/BSA adjusting bolt is covered by the upper cam tower plate, fitted with nine screws and sealed with a gasket.

The fact that the cam tower is on the left side of the engine may be puzzling until you realize that the whole engine is "backwards." As all previous British ohc engines have shifted on the right, the result has been that the transmission input and engine output sprockets have been on the left, and the cam drive therefore on the right. The new 350 shifts on the left, not because the British are admitting that Europeans and Japanese are right after all, but because they have agreed to conform to forthcoming federal motorcycle controls standards in America, which constitutes the bulk of the British market. This means, of course, that the 350's drive side is now on the right, instead of the left.

In one aspect, the 350 seems to have come around to Japanese practice in that the crankpins are opposed 180 degrees, rather than running parallel, which creates the same balance problems you find in a Single. This is to (quote-unquote) reduce vibration at high rpm. A 180-degree configuration moves one side of the piston-crank assembly up while

→

The styling is sleek, the engine hairy and the frame impressive. The new 350s should reach these shores in March.

the other half is moving down, thereby eliminating primary imbalance. But, in a Twin, a 180-degree disposition of crankpins creates a rocking couple, which also may be a source of vibration and stress. Honda's solution to the problem was to add flywheels and support bearings, using the extra engine width created to run the cam drive chain in the cavity between the cylinder barrels of its Twins.

BSA/Triumph's answer is to keep the crankshaft as short as possible by the use of an outside cam drive tower, and slightly smaller bore (Honda's 325-cc Twin is 65 by 50.6mm, while the new Triumph 349-cc Twin is 63 by 56mm). Naturally, moving the pistons, and thus the crankthrows, closer together will diminish the effect of the rocking couple as well as make the crankshaft more rigid by virtue of its shortness. This hopefully precludes the need for extra bearing surfaces, and thus only the two ends of the Triumph 350's crankshaft are supported by ball and roller bearings.

It is probably for this reason that the designers chose to retain the traditional British method of splitting the crankcase vertically. Had they needed extra bearing surfaces, they probably would have gone to horizontally split cases which lend themselves quite well in production to the provision of extra inboard bearing supports. Still, it is hard to argue in favor of vertically split crankcases, particularly with an in-unit transmission, as the horizontally split engine has historically proven itself more oil tight and more easily serviced.

A double-gear pump lubricates the shell-type big ends and also scavenges the dry sump. Oil to the bearings runs first through a large capacity filter with replaceable element. To lubricate the valve gear, the designers have chosen an outside oil line, which is a valid alternative to running a feeder duct through the cylinder barrels, even though it seems somewhat archaic.

The transmission/clutch assembly resembles that of the smooth-shifting "C" series 500 Triumphs, although it now has five speeds instead of four, and is in "mirror" image to its predecessors, having the clutch on the right and the shifting lever on the left. Otherwise, it seems quite the familiar mainshaft/layshaft arrangement, with a horizontal selector plate moving the gears back and forth on their shafts by means of shifting forks. The kick starter is, glory be, on the left side, cranking through the gearbox to turn the engine. A 0.375-in. duplex chain transmits power from the engine to a multi-disc, shock-cushioned wet plate clutch, linked to the mainshaft. Yet another single-row chain links the engine driveshaft with an optional electric starter, nestled on top of the cases behind the cylinder barrel.

A Lucas 110-watt alternator, mounted on the crankshaft drive side, provides current for ignition and lighting. The points are driven off the front cam at the right end. Drive for the tachometer is taken off the crankshaft on the timing side. Near that point, removal of a conically shaped top, which doubles as a pressure relief valve, will expose an oil filter for easy cleaning.

Appearance of so new a British engine overshadows the frame it is carried in, and the rolling gear, both of which are significant improvements in themselves. The frame resembles very closely the triangulated "space" frames in which the potent BSA and Triumph Threes were mounted for running on the AMA road racing circuits last year. If it lives up to its promises, the new 350 should be one of the finest handling production motorcycles ever manufactured in Great Britain. The manufacturers of that country, if conservative in other matters, are unequaled in the design of motorcycle racing chassis.

CONTINUED ON PAGE 80

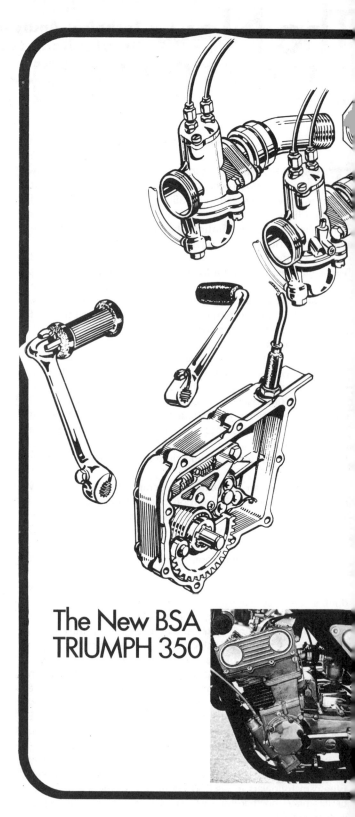

The New BSA TRIUMPH 350

SPECIFICATIONS

Bore/stroke, mm.	63 x 56
Bore/stroke, in.	2.48 x 2.20
Capacity, cc	349
Capacity, cu. in.	21.3
Compression ratio	9.5:1
Bhp @ rpm	34 @ 9000
Engine sprocket teeth	23
Clutch sprocket teeth	52
Gearbox sprocket teeth	17

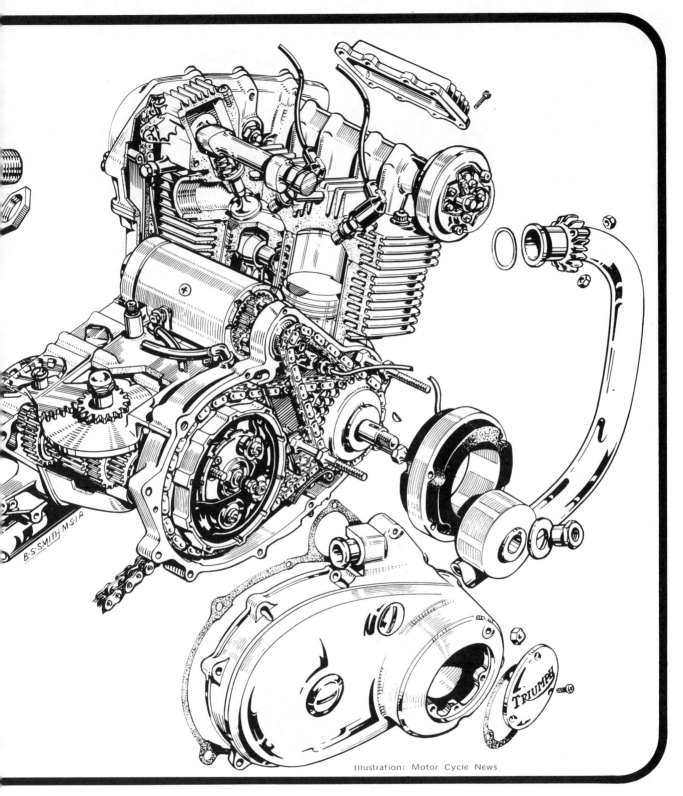

B.S.SMITH M.S.I.A

Illustration: Motor Cycle News

Rear sprocket teeth	....	48
Rpm @ 10 mph (top gear)	....	870
Gear ratio		
5th	....	6.39
4th	....	7.37
3rd	....	9.03
2nd	....	11.48
1st	....	17.1
Carburetor	....	(2) 26-mm Amal Concentric
Primary chain size, in.	....	3/8 duplex
Rear chain size, in.	....	5/8 x 1/4
Tire size, front	....	3.25-18 K70

Tire size, rear	....	3.50-18 K70
Front brake dia./type	....	8in., 2LS
Rear brake dia./type	....	7in., 1LS
Seat height, in.	....	30 1/4
Wheel base, in.	....	58 5/8
Length, in.	....	79 1/2
Width, in.	....	26 3/4
Ground clearance, in.	....	6 7/8
Dry weight, lb.	....	345
Gas (U.S. gal.)	....	2 3/4
Oil (U.S. gal.)	....	3/4
Color/finish	....	Jealous Green

TRIUMPH T-120R BONNEVILLE

The Bonnie Has Always Been A Status-Cycle. The Understated Stud Machine, Representative Of Real Motorcycling. Now It Has Been Rewrapped For The 70s. Does It Make It?

AH, THE BONNEVILLE. It has long been a status symbol with the road rider. Not the same way as with other big-bore machines. A BMW, for example, connotes Engineering, with a capital E. An FLH connotes yet another feeling, that of bigness, luxuriousness, and is the most unabashed symbol of affluent arrival. The Bonneville symbol is a more dynamic thing. If you are a sporting sort of rider, and deem yourself a bit of a jockey, you may buy yourself a stable of intermediate machines with good performance and handling, but you know you're waiting for the day you can buy your Bonnie.

Its image does not jibe with the purist. The Bonneville is more for the guy who would buy a Boss Mustang or a Z28.

Performance-plus, flashiness in a moderate way, and respectable handling. Like the Sportster, the Bonneville is a stud bike, although the two images aren't quite the same. But, in either case, purchase of one or the other indicates "arrival," the coming of the *real* motorcyclist, and *real* motorcycling.

It seems highly unlikely that the designers of the Triumph Big Twin had this image concept in mind when they created the basis for what was to become the Bonneville. That type of marketing acumen didn't exist in the late Thirties. One can only conclude that Triumph really lucked out, because the half-stud, half-racing "Bonneville image" is the very thing that has kept that firm alive and well to this date.

THE ANCESTRAL SPEED TWIN

Triumph's 1938 Speed Twin 500 heralded what was to become the most popular design, and the most plentiful motorcycle of that design, to ever come out of England. The alternately firing, vertical twin-cylinder engine produced 28.5 bhp, and, with a machine weight of 365 lb., provided the sporting enthusiast with an ideal mount. In fact, the 1939 sports version, the Tiger 100, became a popular machine with motorcycle connoisseurs. It featured an individually built, dynamometer-tested engine producing 34 bhp, and had many other "racing-type" features.

1950 was the year of the first Triumph 650 Twin, the Thunderbird. It had a bore/stroke of 71 by 82mm, measurements which still hold today. These husky machines rapidly gained popularity in America, and became favorites with sports minded riders. TT racing proved to be its forte and a look at the record books will probably reveal that more races of this type have been won by 650 Triumphs than any other single machine.

The first Thunderbirds had a sprung hub rear suspension

system which consisted of a huge rear hub with springs inside that provided a couple of inches of travel. It rode better than a rigid frame, but the hubs were heavy, had no dampening characteristics, and were prone to bearing failures. This form of rear suspension was employed on some of Triumph's models until 1954, when a swinging arm frame appeared.

Along with the frame came the new T-110 model, a super-sports version of the Thunderbird. It featured an alloy cylinder head with large valves, high compression pistons and a sports camshaft. At that time, they were about the fastest road bikes around.

Several other 650 models appeared in the ensuing years, including the popular Trophy and TT versions. In fact, until the "Japanese Invasion," big Triumphs were the most popular machines around in most parts of the country.

A REVAMPED PACKAGE

For 1971, Triumph has revamped practically everything on the 650s except the engine/gearbox package, and even a new five-speed gearbox is optional. Still functionally British in appearance, Triumphs have sprouted many modern-day innovations and styling trends. Gone are the familiar front forks and rear wheel hub. Turn signals are now standard equipment, and gracefully tapered silencers with a gradual upsweep adorn the Bonneville. Large, conical wheel hubs housing improved

TRIUMPH T-120R BONNEVILLE

brakes, and a wide dual seat improves rider comfort.

Perhaps the most interesting aspect of the new 650 is the frame. Twin tubes extend from the steering head below the engine, and then up to the top rear suspension mounts. A large diameter central tube holds 3.5 qt. of oil, which does away with the old, separate oil tank. The "spine's" larger size makes for a stronger frame. The engine is firmly bolted directly to the frame at the front and underneath, and steel plates support it at the rear. A flat support anchors it on top. Gusseting at the front of the swinging arm, which pivots on bronze bushes, appears very beefy, but the tubes themselves look rather delicate. Welds are very smooth, and the paint is excellent.

Steering geometry felt just right for normal road riding, with a bit of fast swervery thrown in. Gone is the tendency of earlier Bonnevilles towards understeering; in fact, the new Bonnie feels rather like its little brother, the Triumph T-100 500-cc Twin, which is several pounds lighter. The installation of a 3.25-19 Dunlop K70 tire seems to be the trend these days, and it probably helps smooth out the bumps a little, too. Traction is very good, with no tendency towards side-slipping at low speeds.

ROLLER BEARING STEERING HEAD

Part of the Bonnie's hairline steering and good ride are attributable to the new front fork assembly, which rides in tapered roller bearings. The fork legs feature cast alloy sliders with rubber wipers and internal springs. Full two-way hydraulic dampening and almost 7 in. of fork travel help make them one of the best operating fork assemblies available. Even with two aboard, no bottoming occurs, and there is no annoying clank when they topped out going across railroad tracks or badly surfaced roads.

The rear suspension units are, of course, Girlings, and aside from seeming to have a slightly stiffer spring rate than earlier Bonnevilles, they added immeasurably to the handling and ride. The chrome plated springs are a nice touch, but the damper rods are left exposed, which could cause premature wear of the seals if the machine is ridden in wet or dusty surroundings.

The wheel hubs are very racy in appearance and house an excellent set of brakes. Diameter of the front unit is 8 in. It has twin leading shoes. The pivot arms are pulled toward each other like a BMW and therefore no equalizing rod is used.

A functional airscoop funnels cool air into the drum and carries off excess heat and brake dust. Even after several hard, high speed applications, the front wheel continued to do its share of stopping the machine. The rear wheel is similar in appearance, but the brake drum is an inch smaller in diameter. Although less positive in feel than the front brake, the rear was smooth in operation.

In addition, the rear sprocket may be unbolted for easy gear ratio changes or replacement. One point we don't care for is the rear wheel speedometer drive. It necessitates a long cable, and is less accurate than a speedometer driven from the front wheel.

A FAMILIAR ENGINE

Basically unchanged from last year, the Triumph 650 engine remains one of the Western world's mechanical marvels. It starts easily, vibrates only mildly, and has good power available throughout a wide rpm range. Both ball and roller

bearings support the ends of the crankshaft; plain insert rod bearings and wrist pin bearings provide quiet running and high load carrying capability, and 9:1 compression ratio three-ring pistons take advantage of today's high octane fuels.

A separate camshaft for the intake and exhaust valves makes it possible to have pushrods of equal length, and makes it easy to degree-in the camshafts for optimum performance. Both shafts are gear driven from the crankshaft and ride in sintered bronze bushings. The double-plunger-type oil pump is driven from the inlet shaft, as is the crankcase breather, and the exhaust shaft drives the contact breaker assembly.

A welcome change to the 1971 650s is the addition of four inspection caps on the sides of the rocker boxes. When these caps are removed, a feeler gauge can be inserted to check the valve clearances. This makes it easier to obtain *really* accurate valve clearance settings.

Twin 30-mm Amal concentric carburetors breathe through "tuned" intake tubes which terminate into gauze air filter elements. These are housed in metal boxes under the seat and are very clean looking and stylish. Although the carburetors are fitted with choke slides, we didn't find it necessary to close the lever even on cold mornings. Just make sure the float bowls are liberally primed, the ignition switch is on, and most often the bike will come to life with, at most, two kicks.

A twin-row primary chain is retained to drive the clutch. Adjustment is accomplished via a rubber-faced tension slipper blade under the lower run of the chain. Rubber inserts inside the clutch hub cushion the engine's power impulses and increase the life of the chains and gearbox components. As always, the Triumph's three-spring clutch was easy to operate and didn't slip or drag.

HOW THE GEARBOX WORKS

The Triumph gearbox shifts smoothly and is silent in operation. Shifting is accomplished by a spindle and plunger assembly which pivots a quadrant that in turn moves the cam plate. A spring-loaded index plunger fits into notches in the cam plate for each gear and for neutral. Robust is the keyword; essentially the same gearbox is used in the more powerful 750-cc three-cylinder Trident.

Announced as an optional extra is a five-speed gearbox with a slightly lower first gear, and the rest of the gear ratios closer together. If it shifts as well as the four-speed gearbox, it'll be a winner.   →

Due to the incorporation of the engine oil into the frame, with the resulting large main tube, the gas tank is now slightly bulbous in the front section in order to keep the area between the rider's knees down to a reasonable width and retain the 3.5 gal. capacity. The seat, although very comfortable, is quite high at 34.5 in. Two of our shorter staffers found it impossible to plant both feet squarely on the ground. Another point that vexed us slightly was the unsightly oil pressure indicator sender unit which protrudes from the right side of the crankcase and is covered with an ugly rubber cap. The indicator light is located in a spot (on the back of the headlight shell) which makes it difficult to see when illuminated, except at night. Oil system failures on the large Triumphs are so rare these days, it seems that the indicator could have been left off.

RUBBER-MOUNTED INSTRUMENTS

Rubber is used to mount the handlebars to reduce vibration, and the new-style Smith tachometer and speedometer nestle in their own isolation mounts. Both are quite accurate, but it's beyond us why so many manufacturers (and the Japanese, too) insist on fitting 150-mph speedometers on machines that won't pass the 120-mph mark. Besides being superfluous, the numbers must be made smaller (or fewer must be used) to keep them from being too small to read comfortably.

Another sore point, which we recently found on another British machine, was the new, *improved* Lucas electrical control units/lever holders. These cast aluminum units are very dull in appearance and have sharp plastic blades which must be flicked up or down to operate the turn signals or dip the headlamp. These blades are sharp, of a peculiar shape, and look as though they'd be easy to break off. Two buttons, one above and one below the blade switch, operate the horn and high beam flasher on the left; one button on the right is an engine cutout and the other button is left free for some other function.

The remainder of the electrical system deserves praise. The headlight throws a wide, powerful beam, the horn is suitably loud in volume, and the wiring is very well done. Triumph has taken great pains to rubber-mount the coils, rectifier and battery, and the area under the seat is used to its best advantage to locate these items for easy access. A new four-position ignition and light switch allows the rider to leave his machine parked with the ignition locked off and the parking lights locked on at the same time.

Other nice touches are rubber-mounted front fender braces, the overall excellent quality of finish (both paint and chrome), and precise handling qualities. This machine is one of Triumph's best.

TRIUMPH T-120R BONNEVILLE

SPECIFICATIONS

List price	$1479
Suspension, front	telescopic fork
Suspension, rear	swinging arm
Tire, front	3.25-19
Tire, rear	4.00-18
Brake, front, diameter x width, in.	8 x 1.5
Brake, rear, diameter x width, in.	7 x 1.375
Total brake swept area, sq. in.	68.27
Brake loading, lb./sq. in.	8.2
Engine, type	ohv vertical Twin
Bore x stroke, in., mm	2.79 x 3.23, 71 x 82
Piston displacement, cu. in., cc	40, 649
Compression ratio	9:1
Claimed bhp @ rpm	50 @ 7000
Claimed torque @ rpm, lb.-ft.,	38.5 @ 6000
Carburetion	(2) 30-mm Amal concentric
Ignition	battery and coil
Oil system	double plunger pump, dry sump
Oil capacity, pt.	6
Fuel capacity, U.S. gal.	3.5
Recommended fuel	premium
Starting system	kick, folding crank
Lighting system	12V alternator
Air filtration	gauze
Clutch	multi-disc, wet
Primary drive	duplex chain (2.0)
Final drive	single-row chain (2.47)
Gear ratios, overall:1	
5th	none
4th	4.95
3rd	6.14
2nd	8.36
1st	12.08
Wheelbase, in.	56
Seat height, in.	34.5
Seat width, in.	11.5
Handlebar width, in.	32
Footpeg height, in.	12.2
Ground clearance, in.	6.5
Curb weight (w/half-tank fuel), lb.	399
Weight bias, front/rear, percent	43.5/56.5
Test weight (fuel and rider), lb.	559

TEST CONDITIONS

Air temperature, degrees F	68
Humidity, percent	62
Barometric pressure, in. hg.	29.72
Altitude above mean sea level, ft.	50
Wind velocity, mph	8-10
Strip alignment, relative wind:	

PERFORMANCE

Top speed (actual @ 7400 rpm), mph	112.2
Computed top speed in gears (@ 7000 rpm), mph:	
5th	none
4th	110
3rd	88
2nd	65
1st	45
Mph/1000 rpm, top gear	15.7
Engine revolutions/mile, top gear	3820
Piston speed (@ 7000 rpm), ft./min.	3768
Lb./hp (test wt.)	11.17
Fuel consumption, mpg	48
Speedometer error:	
50 mph indicated, actually	46.9
60 mph indicated, actually	57.6
70 mph indicated, actually	67.7
Braking distance:	
from 30 mph, ft.	30.4
from 60 mph, ft.	140.1
Acceleration, zero to:	
30 mph, sec.	2.9
40 mph, sec.	4.3
50 mph, sec.	4.9
60 mph, sec.	5.8
70 mph, sec.	7.0
80 mph, sec.	10.0
90 mph, sec.	13.9
100 mph, sec.	17.6
Standing one-eighth mile, sec.	8.24
terminal speed, mph	76.33
Standing one-quarter mile, sec.	14.24
terminal speed, mph	92.87

ACCELERATION / ENGINE AND ROAD SPEEDS / RPM X 100

THE MACIAS TRIBSA

A Triumph Lover's Answer To BSA's 500 MX

BY JODY NICHOLAS

The names Macias and Triumph have been synonymous for almost 25 years. As far back as 1948 Danny Macias was a Triumph dealer in Orange County, California. Danny was an active competitor for the four years he owned the shop, but began riding more competition events after he sold it. One year he was high-point rider in TT competition at the now-defunct Console Springs race track, to the east of Los Angeles.

Drag racing, Bonneville salt flats and track racing challenged Danny for many years, and as a master mechanic at Bellflower Cycle Shop he was able to build and tune many highly successful Triumph competition bikes. His two most recent riders are TT champion Skip Van Leeuwen and winner of the 1971 8-mile national at Ascot, Tom Rockwood.

Shortly before the start of the 1971 AMA racing season, Danny was put in charge of the racing departments of the BSA/Triumph combine. The results of his efforts are now history: BSA and Triumph riders took six out of the first ten finishing positions in the AMA national championship series including Dick Mann's grand national championship victory, and runners-up Gene Romero, Jim Rice and Dave Aldana.

Being a former competition rider, Danny enjoys a good "cow-trailing" session every now and then as well as an occasional trip to Mexico (Baja, California) with members of the infamous Gold Star and Antique Four-Stroke Club. In fact, Danny's previous 40- and 30.5-cu. in. Triumphs have proven to be among the most powerful and reliable bikes in the group.

The Tiger 100 engine fits into the B50MX frame with room to spare. Note the special inlet manifold rubber spacer and engine breathers, extensive use of allen screws.

Conical aluminum alloy rear hub is strong, helps reduce unspring weight.

WHAT DOES A Triumph lover do when BSA (Triumph's sister company) builds the most sophisticated and best handling "big banger" motocross four-stroke available today? It's not that Danny Macias doesn't like a Single, he just prefers a Twin; so he grafted a 30.5-cu. in. Triumph Tiger 100 engine into a BSA B50MX chassis and has come up with what must be one of the best handling Triumph 500s in captivity!

Shoehorning the Tiger 100 engine into the BSA frame was a relatively easy job, requiring only the making of special aluminum engine mounting plates. The only other special bits needed for the swap were upswept exhaust pipes that originated on a 500cc Triumph but had to be altered slightly to fit properly. All else on the bike is standard with the exception of the handlebars, the Triumph decal on the gas tank and the progressively wound rear shock springs.

A close look at the Triumph engine won't tell you much about what's inside, but the absence of oil leaks after a hard day's running reflects Danny's careful assembly technique. In fact, the only clues about the inside are the 32mm Amal concentric carburetor, a special rubber intake manifold spacer block and two non-standard engine breathers. One is in the crankcase behind the cylinders and one exits at the clutch case oil filler plug.

Modifications to the engine have been made not only to give slightly increased performance but also to make the engine more reliable and smoother running. Although a 32mm carburetor is fitted, the actual size of the inlet ports was left unchanged at a nominal 28mm. Inlet valves with a head diameter approximately 1/16-in. larger were fitted, but only because they are made of better steel than the standard items. A set of JRS-1 valve springs with alumi-num valve spring retainers, in conjunction with special alloy pushrods, allow high engine rpm without fear of floating the valves.

The standard compression ratio of 9:1 has been lowered to the region of 8:1 for increased engine smoothness and to make the engine happier running on the low octane gas which is abundant in Mexico. A standard camshaft is used. When Danny built the engine the only crankshaft he had around was one he lightened for use in a 500 Triumph road racer several years ago. This makes throttle response a bit quick, but plans to install a standard crank and flywheel have been made.

No changes were made to the transmission or the clutch as both are reliable, but the scarcity of rear sprockets means changing the countershaft sprocket to alter gearing which is too low at present.

Engine weight is less than 20 lb. heavier than a BSA B50MX engine, and slightly over half of that increase is placed on the front wheel. This makes the bike somewhat easier to "steer" than a B50MX. Power is a little sudden with the light flywheel, but is helpful in breaking the rear end loose and into a slide if you feel like practicing half-mile racing.

In order to make the exhaust quiet (and the bike "forest legal") a spark arrester/muffler was fitted. Very little top-end horsepower has been lost and mid-range power delivery is slightly stronger and decidedly smoother. There is no feeling of "caminess" in the rev-range, making the bike very predictable and easy to ride.

Word just received here at the Cycle World offices has it that similar machines will be available from local Triumph dealers in the future. Yes, Virginia, there is something distinctly exciting about a Twin! ◘

New 350

CONTINUED FROM PAGE 70

Basic frame configuration of the 350 is a full double loop, with an important addition. From mid-frame, near the swinging arm pivot, two triangulating members run closely parallel to the cylinders and over the engine to the steering head; this creates a compact, rigid engine bay, and reduces the possibility of mid-frame flex.

Suspension and rolling gear, all-new, and shared with the entire BSA and Triumph lines, should do much to complement the chassis. The internal spring front forks have lightweight alloy sliders and offer two-way hydraulic dampening with 6.75-in. travel. The sliders and the new aluminum conical front and rear brake hubs should do much to reduce unsprung weight, allowing the wheels to more closely follow undulations in the road. At front, the brake is an 8-in. double leading shoe unit, with each shoe adjustable by "snail" cams. The 7-in. rear brake consists of one leading and one trailing shoe operated by a floating cam.

We had a chance to sample these suspension units and brakes on some of the larger BSA and Triumph models, and found that they work quite well.

Other than the horsepower figures, the manufacturers have released no "teasers" in the form of performance claims. It's just as well, as the announced gearing, cranked into a slip-stick along with the announced peak rpm figure, gives us an ample prediction of top speed performance that should be accurate to within 5 mph. The claimed performance is 34 bhp at 9000 rpm. With a 6.39 overall ratio the to gear rpm is 870 at 10 mph. If th machine will pull to peak rpm in to gear, which it should with 34 bhp, will run between 98 and 103 mph fla out. Quarter-mile acceleration rur should yield trap speeds in the neighbo hood of 80 to 85 mph from a standir start. This speculation, of course, contingent on how correctly the de signers have geared the machine. If the have, then we may presume that th 350, as delivered, is in a relatively mi state of tune. This thought would b borne out by the throat size of the tw Amal Concentric carburetors fitted t the machine—a modest 26mm each.

The definitive figures will come t light when the 350 undergoes the rigor of a CYCLE WORLD road test. I should be exciting.